Be All You Can Be

BE ALL YOU CAN BE

David Augsburger

CREATION HOUSE
CAROL STREAM, ILLINOIS

© 1970 by Creation House. All rights reserved.

Published by Creation House, 499 Gundersen Drive,
Carol Stream, Illinois 60187
Distributed in Canada: Beacon Distributing Ltd.,
104 Consumers Drive, Whitby, Ontario L1N 5T3
Distributed in Australia: Oracle Australia, Ltd.,
18-26 Canterbury Road, Heathmont, Victoria 135

All quotations of Scripture, unless otherwise noted, are
from J.B. Phillips' *The New Testament in Modern English,*
and are reprinted by permission of the Macmillan
Company, New York.

ISBN 0-88419-013-7
Library of Congress Catalog Card No. 76-131444
Printed in the United States of America

First printing—August 1970

New Leaf Library Edition
First printing—March 1977

CONTENTS

Chapter   **Page**

1   What is the Best You Could Be?   9

2   Do You Know How Much You Are Worth?   15

3   Can You Believe the Best of Your Friends?   21

4   Can You Draw the Best from Your Anger?   27

5   Can You Get the Best of Your Fears?   33

6   Can You Do Your Best in Conversation?   39

7   Can You Make the Most of What You Have?   49

8   Can You Be Your Best in Failure?   59

9   Can You Make the Most of Your Sexuality?   67

10   Can You Be Your Best in Marriage?   73

11   Can You Be Your Best in Parenthood?   81

12   Can You Be Your Best in Love?   91

13   Can You Be Your Best in Human Relations?   99

14   Can You Be Your Best When Mistreated?   109

15   Can You Be Your Best in Forgiveness?   117

16   Can You Be Your Best in Joy?   127

     Notes   136

CHAPTER ONE

What is the Best You Could Be?

It has to happen just when you've muffed your piece of work at the lathe. You look both ways to see if anyone saw—and then you see him. Your foreman. Right behind your left shoulder. And frowning. And you feel a bit less than your best.

Or it's when you're dining alone in the restaurant. You've just caught your elbow and soaked your tie with soup, and then you hear her voice. You look up into her smile, your jaw slack with surprise. Hardly at your best.

How often it happens. We're caught with our worst foot first. When we want most to succeed!

And even more often we fail ourselves in those many little ways that mar our attempts at living. And we find ourselves forced to admit how far short we come, short even of our own standards of maturity. What could be more welcome than to always be at your best? Or is that dreaming the impossible dream?

What if you could be the best you could possibly become?

Be everything that's in you? Be all you can be? You might be able to, you know.

Perhaps it's too late to be your best in your vocation. . .

I know a man with a beautiful voice, a resonant, rich mahogany kind of baritone. He's a farmer. He sings as he works. To his unresponsive animals. He might have moved the hearts of millions, but. . .

I know a painter with an artisan's touch. By night he copies old masters in intricate miniature. He's a carpenter by trade. His gift of painting will never be able to blossom into service for men as it might have, if. . .

There are ghettos teeming with people who might have been, if only the opportunity had not been denied them.

There are suburbs stagnating with people who could have been if only they had not rejected open opportunity.

But even when many opportunities are past—educational, vocational—the privilege of becoming is still open.

You can be the best you can be—as a person. You can become a person of integrity, of maturity, a person of dignity. You can be you. Truly you.

A man of perfect integrity? No, but a man whose self and soul are rightly integrated with both God and man.

A man of perfect maturity? No, rather a man who is constantly maturing, a man in the open-ended process of maturing.

Why talk of a "maturing man" instead of a "mature man"?

One: Life is not school, where you learn the right answers and graduate to maturity. Life is a continuous experience of growth and development. Adults never lose their capacity to learn.

Two: The important age measurement for a man is not chronological, be he seventeen or seventy-seven. Age must be marked psychologically, emotionally, spiritually. How old are you as a person and as a personality? Not all adults (by age) are adult (in character). Some never grow up. And some are wise beyond their years.

Three: We never arrive at maturity and heave that "well-that's-all-there-is-to-that" sigh of relief. If we think we've arrived, we've simply stopped growing. We've given up on life. We've copped out. "Arrested development" psychologists call it. It accounts for a lot of men with childish emotions, baby-soft feelings, and toddler angers. It explains some of those women who, though forty-six, still dress like eighteen, flirt like seventeen, and dream of being sweet sixteen forever.

But the maturing person, at any age (as numbered by years) is constantly reaching out for maturity in personality and personhood. He is growing, maturing, becoming all that he can be. He is enroute from infancy to adulthood.

The human being is born ignorant, and with no need for any knowledge except how to survive. Later he will discover his second great need—the need not only for survival but for significance. Man needs meaning as well as meat. But when you see an adult-aged person living—working—valuing only survival, you see an infant. If his influence and responsibility call for more knowledge but he makes no effort to get it, he is an infant. If he feels his present store of knowledge is enough for life, he is a child.

The human being is born irresponsible, caring only for himself and his own satisfaction. "All children are essentially criminal," wrote one pessimistic philosopher a century ago. And that is true in a sense. Humans are safe only if they are as weak in powers of execution as they are in powers of understanding. Nothing is more treacherous than a grown-old child.

The human being is born self-centered, unable to communicate, unable to relate to others, unable—yet—to be human in love and understanding. Toward this he must grow in constant maturing. He is born with a vague capacity to be sexual; he must learn to gather up this diffuse drive and direct it to a creative end. All of his maturing will be in tension with this self-centeredness that afflicts him.

So, the maturing person is a person who is growing from self-centeredness, selfish irresponsibility, and childish ignorance toward the wisdom of responsible, loving relationships with his fellows and his Creator. He is mature to the degree that he relates himself affirmatively to God and man.

Jesus said that flawlessly. Twenty centuries of man's knowledge explosion failed to improve on it. The highest good for man is. . .

" 'Thou shalt love the Lord thy God with all thy heart, and with all thy soul and with all thy mind.' This is the first and great commandment. And there is a second like it: 'Thou shalt love thy neighbour as thyself' " (Matt. 22:37-39, Phillips).

That is the goal of a maturing man. But how? How do we live once we agree on the highest goal?

To be all that we can be, we need a pattern for living, a style of life bound up in a person. We've got to see what living can be.

A person? One person? Who could it be? Who but Jesus Christ? I know that sounds so hopelessly religious. So many patterns for living have been constructed by men, and they've attached Christ's name to them in human vanity. All too often they've abused and distorted the flawless example of Christ to make Him look like their own mirror image. To make Him look like their kind of guy. No wonder many men have shouted, "Jesus, yes; systems, no!" or "Jesus, yes; Christianity, no." If I were forced to accept the common Christianity of today, I'd shout the same rejection.

It is Jesus that I want, not religion. Is that at all true for you?

It is Jesus, the man who showed us life, liberty, peace, love, forgiveness, happiness; the man who showed us God, who is the only guide and goal for the truly maturing man. He should be. He was and is God.

But He was also a human—a human like no other—who showed us what a man can be. He was man—with a body

12

that ached with hunger and desire. He was human—with the need for friendship and loving acceptance. He was sensitive, with feelings of both affection and anger, with love for good and hatred for evil, with laughter and tears. He was what we ought to be. What in our best moments we want to be. What we can be—with His life-changing help.

What does this mean for our maturing?

One: Life is not school; it is continuous growth in following a mature pattern of living—Jesus Christ.

Indeed this is your calling. For Christ suffered for you and left you a personal example, and wants you to follow in his steps (I Peter 2:21, Phillips).

Two: Life is measured by growth in maturity, not by the seasons and the years. We grow toward the maturity of Jesus, to be. . .

. . .built up until the time comes when, in the unity of common faith and common knowledge of the Son of God, we arrive at real maturity—that measure of development which is meant by "the fulness of Christ". We are not meant to remain as children. . .But we are meant to hold firmly to the truth in love, and to grow up in every way into Christ. . .to. . .full maturity in love (Eph. 4:13, 14a, 15, 16b, Phillips).

Three: Life is a constant pilgrimage. Life is maturing as we move enroute from infancy and its self-imprisonment to the adulthood of loving service. As St. Paul, one of history's most avid maturers once said:

Yet, my brothers, I do not consider myself to have "arrived", spiritually, nor do I consider myself already perfect. But I keep going on, grasping ever more firmly that purpose for which Christ Jesus grasped me. My brothers, I do not consider myself to have fully grasped it even now. But I do concentrate on this: I leave the past behind and with hands outstretched to whatever lies ahead I go straight for the goal—my reward the honour of my high calling by God in Christ Jesus.

All of us who are spiritually adult should set ourselves this sort of ambition, and if at present you cannot see this, yet you will find that this is the attitude which God is leading you to adopt (Phil. 3:12-15, Phillips).

CHAPTER TWO

Do You Know How Much You Are Worth?

How much is a man worth?

Some men attempt to answer that question off the top of their heads.

"There's a great difference in value between one man and another," a young collegian told me. He was a political science senior in an eastern university, certain of his answers and education. The miles slipped by as we talked of world need and world concerns.

"There's a vast difference in value," he continued, "between an educated, civilized western man from an advanced culture, and a bushman from the wilds of Borneo. One of us is worth any quantity of them."

"I must take the other side," I replied, "I believe that every man is of equal worth."

"Of equal worth? Then you agree with tyrants, despots, and all those who consider the masses as one faceless horde? You side with Mao Tse-tung and his Red Guards who think all life is cheap?"

"No, no; you miss the whole point. Those you mention insist that man is of equal worthlessness. But I stand with Christ who considered all men of equal *worth.*"

What is the worth of a man? Or has he none until he earns it? Or has he worth only in terms of his property or possessions? Or is his worth bound up in his culture or education?

How much is a man worth? If you think long about that question, think long enough to get personal about it, you discover it can't be answered by theories.

A man has to find an answer to it in his heart. An answer that satisfies his own heart, an answer that gives him heart enough to get along with his fellowmen.

A man can lose his own sense of worth so quickly if! If he has posited it in his work, talent, race, position or possessions.

If he gained his sense of worth from his work, what then? If he's replaced by mechanization, he may feel like the man who complained, "If I'd been replaced by a computer I could accept it, but by a tiny transistor?"

If he's denied his job by being dropped in favor of a younger, a better educated, a more efficient person, his feelings of his own importance may crumble.

Or if society has denied him any sense of worth because of his race, if his community tells him to be black is bad, Indian is evil, Mexican is undesirable, he may hate himself and lose all sense of significance.

Or if his world loves only the young and beautiful, he may grow to hate the age spots on his hands, the crow's-feet at his eyes, the whitening of his hair and lose his sense of worth in his most important years.

Do you know how much you are worth?

No, not by the decimal point in your fortune.

No, not by the number of earning years ahead, by the mileage still in you.

No, not by the phony, fraudulent values passed around by your society, community, or even family.

But have you discovered how much you are truly worth as a man? A man created by God? A man made in His image?

Dignity is your birthright.

Even if men have maligned your race, made you lose face, or have stolen your rightful place in life.

You have a birthright to claim. Dignity.

You were made in the image of God. The purpose of human creation was, in God's own words:

"Let us make man in our image, after our likeness; and let them have dominion". . .So God created man in his own image, in the image of God he created him (Gen. 1:26a, 27a, RSV).

Dignity is your birthright. You possess a free, self-conscious, thoughtful, moral mind and personality. You are next of kin to God Himself. He is our nearest relative. Not the animal world about us.

There is so much—much more to man than the mere physical animal character of his body. There is spirit, person, intelligence, creativity, moral judgment, freedom of choice, and self-understanding.

We bear the stamp, the signature of our Creator. Eternity is written in our hearts. We sense it as we realize that nothing in this earth can ever truly satisfy us. We feel it when we recognize that we will never be able to fulfill all that the Creator has built into us. We recognize it when we just can't forget those basic questions—"Who am I? Why am I? Where am I going?" Of course, we can't silence them. They run in the family. God's family.

God is our next of kin.

Don't question your own worth, whatever rises. Don't doubt your own value. You are a man of dignity. True, there may be moments when you mentally punish yourself for not measuring up to what you could be, or moments when you hate yourself for failing when success might have been yours. But even at such times of depression you need not despair of yourself. Not only is dignity your birthright. . .

Liberty is your inheritance. The liberty to become a person worthy of your own respect. The liberty to be an individual who accepts himself, understands his frustrations, and climbs away from them step by difficult step.

You are a person, meant to experience undisputed dignity. But where the evil of the world around you and the sinfulness of the world within you have destroyed the heart of it all, you can be set free to become.

That is what Jesus Christ's life—death—and re-life are all about.

He lived among us to show in flesh and blood what a man can be. He showed us the true worth of character and compassion, of flawless honesty and loving openness. He showed us MAN.

He died among us, at our hand, to show the supreme value He placed on every person. He died—freely, voluntarily submitting Himself to absorb the hatred and hostilities of men—and in so doing He took on Himself the responsibility for every man's evil.

God died for the liberation of man from sin. There is no man for whom God did not die. No man has ever lived who was not involved in the execution of Jesus Christ. We killed Him, you and I. He died because we were what we were.

Now then: No man for whom Christ died can ever be considered worthless, insignificant, of no value. If there was dignity given us in creation—there is double dignity given us by our redemption through Christ's death.

And now, liberty is your privilege. God accepts you. He showed it by coming to be a friendly example of life as it can be in Jesus. God forgives you. He paid the full painful cost of forgiving—that's substituting Himself to bear His own anger at our evil so that we may be set free, right? He puts us at liberty. At liberty to be our true selves.

Dignity is our birthright, liberty our new inheritance, and ...*Humanity is our responsiblity.*

To be human to ourselves and to our brothers.

To ourselves, we owe acceptance.

We have no reason to rise in pride, or to sink in depression. We can now afford to be what we are before God. At peace with Him—at peace with ourselves.

The Bible says:

Don't cherish exaggerated ideas of yourself or your importance, but try to have a sane estimate of your capabilities by the light of the faith that God has given to you all (Romans 12:3, Phillips).

To be human, we owe acceptance to our fellow humans as well.

No man, made in the image of God, for whom Christ died can ever be to us—an enemy.

No man, with the dignity of creation, with the liberty offered by Christ's liberation can be to us an object of hatred, discrimination or scorn.

One human life is of more value than a world of gain.

One human life is the highest unit of value in the universe.

Your life is of immeasurable, inconceivable worth.

Humanity—to be a true human before God and to treat all others as such—is our responsiblity.

As the Bible says it:

As, therefore, God's picked representatives of the new humanity, purified and beloved of God himself, be merciful in action, kindly in heart, humble in mind. Accept life, and be most patient and tolerant with one another, always ready to forgive if you have a difference with anyone. Forgive as freely as the Lord has forgiven you. And, above everything else, be truly loving, for love is the golden chain of all the virtues (Col. 3:12-14, Phillips).

CHAPTER THREE

Can You Believe the Best of Your Friends?

Why should you believe a word I say?

And in return, why should I believe you?

Come to think of it, why should you and I believe anyone else? We've been hurt often enough. Let down too many times. Why trust another?

Must we learn to take everything we hear with a grain — or twenty — of salt? Or have we become all too uptight? Too closed up to each other? Too safe in our retreat into our fears?

Can you believe — even your friends?

There's a revealing little parable of three little turtles. They were going out one summer afternoon for a country picnic. One carried a basket with the sandwiches, relishes and desserts. The second, the jug with the turtle-ade. The third — nothing. Just then they felt the first splat of raindrops on their shells.

"We can't have a picnic without an umbrella," said the first. "Who will go back for one?" They quickly odd-manned, and the empty-handed one was chosen.

"I won't go," he said. "As soon as I leave, you'll eat all the food, drink all the turtle-ade, and cut me out of everything, right?"

"Wrong," they say, "we'll wait for you, no matter how long!"

"No matter how long?"

"No matter how long!"

At last he turned back and they sat waiting. . .an hour, two, four. . .a day, two days, a week. Two weeks went by when one turtle turned to the other to say:

"Maybe we should go ahead with the picnic?"

Just then the voice of the third little turtle came from the bushes behind them.

"If you do, I won't go," he said.

That's us too, isn't it? Protecting ourselves against being let down. Shoring up ourselves against being turned down. Withdrawing into ourselves lest we be put down. Hardly daring to venture out in trust.

Do you dare to trust others?

Some of our fears may simply be the "better safe than sorry" sort of caution that has become almost standard equipment for existence today. So we say, "Yes, I'll trust you—if you prove to be trustworthy." Or, "Yes, I'll trust you, but only this far."

Others of our fears may be of the "once burned, twice shy" variety. "Fooled me once, shame on you; fooled me twice, shame on me," we say, and safely distrust one and all.

And then there are those strangely withdrawn fears that grow into suspicions. Suspicions can be based on fact and eventually become reality. But more often they are nothing more than the tortured fears of a mind slowly being tyrannized by anxiety.

Once we begin to fear another, we may explain any and all circumstances as indications of the other person's evil intrigue. "He's avoiding me," we say when we haven't met recently. (Usually there's been no opportunity.) "He's shunning me, ignoring me," we say when we pass on the highway and see no response to our nod. (With both cars doing 60, we pass at 120 m.p.h.) "He's got something against me," we conclude. "He's plotting against me, conspiring to hurt me." Anxiety, when it has conceived, brings forth suspicion; and suspicion, when it is finished, brings forth paranoia (the mental illness with total fear of everyone and everything.)

The maturing man reaches out in trust to his fellow humans instead of withdrawing in fear. One of the most basic tests of maturity is—can a man relate himself affirmatively to his fellowmen? Can he trust? Can he believe another? Can he believe in another? Can he accept others? Can he love his fellowmen?

Trust—belief—acceptance—love. They're one continuous process, you know. One interlocking chain of positive steps toward our fellowmen.

How do we summon the strength to take those steps toward others? To risk being hurt by placing faith in persons who may turn on us?

We cannot go back and change the past which makes us cautious. We can't become the little children once more who automatically give complete faith to anyone. Nor do we want to. We won't be able to erase the scars of betrayal and pretend our trust has never been stabbed in the back.

But we can begin from where we are. Now.

How? By beginning at the core of the problem. By dealing with the basis of trust, not just the practice of giving trust. By working at this basis, the ability to love.

Each of us has a certain potential for giving love. God has gifted us with this capacity for affection towards our fellowmen. The Bible points this out saying:

To you whom I say, let us go on loving one another, for love comes from God. Every man who truly loves is God's son and has some knowledge of him (I John 4:7, Phillips).

And love wants to trust. Love can't help but move a person towards placing all possible faith in another; as the Bible says it:

This love of which I speak is slow to lose patience—it looks for a way of being constructive. It is not possessive: it is neither anxious to impress nor does it cherish inflated ideas of its own importance.

Love has good manners and does not pursue selfish advantage. It is not touchy. It does not keep account of evil or gloat over the wickedness of other people. On the contrary, it is glad with all good men when truth prevails.

Love knows no limit to its endurance, no end to its trust, no fading of its hope; it can outlast anything. It is, in fact, the one thing that still stands when all else has fallen (I Cor. 13:4-8, Phillips).

But is total trust the automatic result of love? No. Hardly. To give love to another is not always the same as giving trust. Trust is one of the usual results of a man's strength—to love. But there may be times when it is the more loving thing to withhold trust.

A man who knows the real nature of the evil that is in us all does not take a naive "all is lovely in a world of pretty people who are good at heart" view of his fellowmen. He does not place his trust in humans—he gives trust to them. His fundamental faith is reserved for God and God alone. God alone deserves it. But because of his faith in God he can afford to give trust to others, knowing that betrayals from our fellowmen can be expected, can be survived, can be forgiven. So he gives trust.

Where trust is at all possible, is at all deserved, the man who loves his neighbor gives trust eagerly.

Where trust may seem improbable, and unlikely to be deserved, the man who lives by the indiscourageable love of God extends it to the other even when it seems likely of being misused.

If there is any hope that our trust may be the one link the other has to life, then love gives trust. If there is any reason to believe that the gift of trust may release the other to be worthy of trust, then love extends it.

We who choose to live by the love of Christ give trust—or withhold it—not in self-defense, not to protect ourselves, but to help. "How can I help my fellowman best?" we ask. "How can I help him be all that he can be?"

And in that action of love, we ourselves begin to become all that we can be in true maturing.

Trust for another—

—believes the best of a friend until it is proven otherwise.

—wishes the best for an enemy, though he deserves otherwise.

—silences all gossip about another until the truth can be seen to be true.

—refuses to accept rumors which the bearer will not confirm with a "Yes, you may quote me" guarantee of good faith.

—takes the initiative in giving a fallen man a second chance at life.

—offers a listening ear and an understanding heart to others no matter what they have been or done.

—gives genuine forgiveness to those who betray him without waiting for their repayment or even their request.

—offers love—self-sacrificial, self-forgetful love—to all those about them.

Note how the Bible puts it:

Let us have no imitation Christian love. Let us have a genuine break with evil and a real devotion to good. Let us have real warm affection for one another as between brothers, and a willingness to let the other man have the credit. . .And as for those who try to make your life a misery, bless them. Don't curse, bless. Share the happiness of those who are happy, and the sorrow of those who are sad. Live in harmony with each other. Don't become snobbish but take a real interest in ordinary people. Don't become set in your own opinions. Don't pay back a bad turn by a bad turn, to anyone. *See that your public behaviour is above criticism. As far as your responsibility goes, live at peace with everyone (Romans 12:9, 10, 14-18, Phillips).*

Impossible? No. Very possible. Not all at once, but step by maturing step as we move toward the flawless example of Jesus. The one who loved without limit, and trusted without safety catches.

To Nicodemus, a probable spy from His enemies, He gave loving attention and a gift of gentle guidance.

To His disciples who betrayed Him in one way or another, He gave loving acceptance that never flinched or faltered.

To the adultress, brought still blushing from the bed of some man who ran and left her to be stoned by the religious vultures, He said, "Neither do I condemn thee, go and sin no more."

To troubled, torn, discouraged, defeated men from all walks of life He offered trust. Loving trust. And through it, a bridge to new life.

So must we. We who pledge to know Christ truly and follow Him daily to a life of true maturity. In a life of daily maturing.

Can you believe the best of your friends?

Your answer may be your next step toward the wholeness of love in life!

Toward maturity!

CHAPTER FOUR

Can You Draw the Best from Your Anger?

How well do you use your anger?

You try not to use it at all?

What a waste. What a waste of inner strength that life needs so badly.

Anger may be one of your greatest sources of inner power, one of your most important personal assets. To let it go un-used is to rob yourself of much needed energy.

All too many people look at anger as a tragic flaw in their personality, as a weakness that should be denied, hidden, and disowned. And, above all else, anger must never be allowed to show its face.

But anger is one of the most virile muscles of a man's mind. One of the strongest sinews of the soul. He who is without it has a crippled personality, a maimed mind.

True, anger may be the most destructive and disruptive force in a man's life. If given free rein it will ravage his friendships, betray his loves, and brutalize the personalities of those in range of its explosion.

But anger can be a creative, constructive force that drives a man to achievements and accomplishments that would be utterly impossible without it.

Anger is a vital, valid, natural emotion. As an emotion, it is in itself neither right nor wrong. The rightness or wrongness depends on the reason for your anger and on the way it is released and exercised.

The question is not, "Is anger right or wrong?" but, "How can I be angry about the right things, for the right reasons, in the right way?"

L. E. Maxwell, Bible scholar and long-time principal of Prairie Bible Institute in Alberta, once wisely wrote: "We have not only the right to be angry, but at certain situations, we cannot be right unless we are angry, if angry rightly."

It is a major step toward maturing when a man is able to be honest about his anger emotions, accept them for what they are, and begin to turn them toward what they can become.

Maturity is accepting one's temper tendency without considering it a curse, but saying instead, "I've been given a warm responsiveness of personality." Then let it become that by the help of God.

Maturity is accepting one's hostile feelings without shame and guilt, but saying instead, "I've been gifted with a profound capacity for concern and compassion for the evils of our world." Let your anger become that through the transformation God works in us.

This is not to excuse one moment of childish hostility or petty anger over self-centered matters. Such angers and temper flare-ups must be suppressed for the moment—for the safety of others, and then expressed through honest discussion with those involved, or confessed to an understanding counselor or friend. Then they can be forgiven and you can be freed from their power.

But that does not include all anger.

Righteous anger, just anger, compassionate anger can be

ours. That is anger turned from destructive ends to constructive purposes.

British Christian A. Powell Davies in his book *The Temptation to Be Good,* writes these penetrating words:

That is one of the truly serious things that has happened to the multitude of so-called ordinary people. They have forgotten how to be indignant. This is not because they are overflowing with human kindness, but because they are morally soft and compliant. When they see evil and injustice, they are pained but not revolted. They mutter and mumble; they never cry out. They commit the sin of not being angry.

Yet their anger is the one thing above all others that would make them count. If they cannot lead crusades or initiate reforms, they can at least create the conditions in which crusades can be effectual and reforms successful. The wrath of the multitude could bring back decency and integrity into public life; it could frighten the corrupt demagogue into silence and blast the rumormonger into oblivion. It could give honest leaders a chance to win.[1]

That is the anger we need. Anger that breathes itself throughout our view of life and our concern for our fellowmen. Such anger is pure optimism, as George Wald, Nobel prize winner in biology, Harvard professor, and spokesman for many concerns of today's youth, writes perceptively:

I am temperamentally an optimist. My optimism now takes the form of anger, and in a choice between despair and anger, anger is the optimistic attitude, because you don't cop out; you keep working on it, and I like to think I'm so angry that that is what keeps me happy.

Anger is an optimistic attitude. It says things could be better if only enough of us cared enough to do something. And something could be—can be—must be done. Despair is its true opposite. Despair is angry pessimism. It is hostility without hope.

The anger we need is that inner burning drive to see

wrongs righted, to see justice practiced all about us, to see more honesty, fairness, truth, and genuine goodness in ourselves.

Christ knew and exercised the emotion of anger. For example, when the scribes and Pharisees, those legalistic, uncaring spectators, stood poised like vultures to criticize Christ's free service to others, He looked angrily at their leering smiles.

He was angered by their rigid, unfeeling slavery to unjust traditions. As Mark tells the story:

> Then he said to them, "Is it right to do good on the Sabbath day, or to do harm? Is it right to save life or to kill?" There was a dead silence. Then Jesus, deeply hurt as he sensed their inhumanity, looked round in anger at the faces surrounding him, and said to the man, "Stretch out your hand!" And he stretched it out, and the hand was restored as sound as the other one (Mark 3:4-6a, Phillips).

Christ's anger was raised by men who should have known compassion, could have cared for other's needs, but did not, simply because they would not. His was anger over principles of right and wrong, of love and indifference, and persons and personalities.

Christ had no kind words to say about anger that is directed at people. Hear His words from the Sermon on the Mount.

> I say to you that anyone who is angry with his brother must stand his trial; anyone who contemptuously calls his brother a fool must face the supreme court; and anyone who looks down on his brother as a lost soul is himself heading straight for the fire of destruction (Matt. 5:22, Phillips).

"Anger and insult alike well deserve the punishment they get," He said.

Christ refused the anger which broods, which will not forget, which refuses to be pacified, and seeks for revenge.

30

Christ's own anger was never motivated by personal abuse. He did not grow angry because men ignored or even attacked Him. Calvary called forth only the word of forgiving love.

But wrong done to others, the abuse of the weak and helpless, ignited His indignation.

Speaking of those who abuse the weak and helpless, He said: "It were better for [a man] that a millstone were hanged about his neck, and he cast into the sea, than that he should offend one of these little ones" (Luke 17:2).

Christ's anger was selfless; it was the anger of love. Anger and love are compatible, you know. In fact, a love that is angerless is as worthless as anger that is without love.

Such anger is to be commended. Commended cautiously, of course, because anger is so easily corrupted and in turn corrupts the angry man. So, when the Bible encourages anger, it does it only with ironclad safeguards.

"Be ye angry and sin not," says the Bible.

If you are angry, be sure that it is not out of wounded pride or bad temper. Never go to bed angry—don't give the devil that sort of foothold. Let there be no more resentment, no more anger or temper, no more violent self-assertiveness, no more slander and no more malicious remarks. Be kind to each other, be understanding. Be as ready to forgive others as God for Christ's sake has forgiven you (Eph. 4:26, 27, 31-32, Phillips).

That is a very helpful set of guidelines. Summarized it says:

1. Be angry, but beware—you are never more vulnerable than when in anger. Self-control is at an all-time low, reason decreases, common sense usually forsakes you.
2. Be angry, but be aware—that anger quickly turns bitter, it sours into resentment, hatred, malice, evil temper and even violence unless it is controlled by love.
3. Be angry, but only to be kind. Only when anger is motivated by love of your brother, by love of what is right

for people, oy what is called from you by love for God, is it constructive, creative anger.

How do we fulfill this in day-to-day living? Here are a few suggestions: slow down your temper, delay your anger, set a later time for settling it after your emotions cool. Always settle it on schedule, put it off while you do a long slow burn. Keep close tab. Balance your anger ledger at the end of each day. "Don't let the sun go down upon your wrath."

Be honest about your anger. Do talk it out. Examine your motives. Be critical of your anger emotions.

And pray. Ask God for strength to replace your old reasons for anger with new concerns about things that truly matter. Confess the self-centeredness that once prompted your temper, let Jesus Christ take that central place in your mind and will, and then put your anger emotions into His control.

Turn them into deep feelings about justice, fairness, truth and service to others.

As was true for St. Paul, let those deep inner springs of emotion — courage, compassion, deep conviction and anger be turned from destructive ends (the persecution and murder of others in flaming anger) to constructive ministry (the great vision and service of giving Christ's new life to men of all races and nations).

Draw the best from your anger. Your greatest weakness may conceal your greatest strength.

Make the most of your anger. Turn it from selfish defensiveness to selfless compassion.

As did Jesus! So must we.

CHAPTER FIVE

Can You Get the Best of Your Fears?

During most of your conscious life, you have been prey to fears of one kind or another, right? And the times when a gray shadow of dread of one sort or another was not in the air have been few, right?

How can I assume so much when we hardly know each other?

Because fear is an unavoidable part of us all. It came as standard equipment at birth—we are born with two fears: fear of falling and fear of loud noises. From these two starters, our fears have multiplied like mice in a cheesehouse.

Some of these fears are indispensable. We need them to survive. But others are the sort that must be mastered or else!

Can you get the best of your fears?

Draw the very best from the fears that are normal and necessary?

And get the best—in victory—over the fears that are abnormal and unnecessary?

That is one of the most crucial questions of maturing. To be all you can be, fear must come under your control!

Sorting your fears may pose little problem to you, but a simple guideline may be — Is this fear one that is common to others as a simple form of self-protection? Does this fear sound reasonable when I explain it to another? And does it have positive results?

Useful fear, constructive fear can be best identified by examining its results. "Fear is creative when it results in appropriate and suitable actions. Fear is destructive when it poisons the mind against others or paralyzes the person so that he cannot do anything." [1]

And if you should suspect your fear of being abnormal . . .test yourself by asking. . .

"Do I stall in the middle of work because my mind is suddenly preempted by fear? Do I find myself often preoccupied by one worry after another? Do my fears disturb my sleep? Do I avoid being part of a group or gathering because of fear? Does fear keep me from enjoying the day-to-day experiences of life?"

If you answer "yes" to any of these questions, it is time for your to get the best of your fears by facing them openly and attempting to rid yourself of them.

A young doctor who had grown up in a home full of fears found himself so infected with worry and anxiety that he could be of no help to anyone else. (Having parents who are always afraid, nervously tense, apprehensive and worried can taint a child's emotions for life, unless he finds help).

So the young doctor, stymied by fears, discovered that he had no health to offer, no help to give. So he poured out his problem to one of his medical professors. The wise old doctor said:

"Son, you can be healed. There is only one Physician who can heal you, but He has a healing potency in His touch. You go to Him. He keeps office in the New Testament and His name is Jesus Christ. You put your life in His hands and

He will heal you of your fears."

That young doctor found healing not in serum or capsule, but in words—the words of the Bible; in faith—faith in Jesus Christ; and in love—the love of Christ within his fear-torn soul.

Jesus Christ has much to say about replacing our fears with faith and love. In His Sermon on the Mount He pointed out how useless, how helpless worry can be.

Listen to His words:

"That is why I say to you, don't worry about living— wondering what you are going to eat or drink, or what you are going to wear. Surely life is more important than food, and the body more important than the clothes you wear. So don't worry and don't keep saying, 'What shall we eat, what shall we drink or what shall we wear?'! Don't worry at all then about tomorrow. Tomorrow can take care of itself! One day's trouble is enough for one day" (Matt. 6:25, 31, 34, Phillips).

One: There are two things you should never worry about. The things you can't help—and the things you can! Why worry about what you cannot help? It will do no good! Why worry about what you can help? If you can help, do it and do it now.

Two: There are two days you should never worry about. Yesterday and tomorrow. Yesterday is gone forever. You cannot correct its blunders, right its mistakes, undo its deeds, silence its speech. So why worry about the past? Confess its blunders to the only One who can forgive them. Tomorrow is not yet. Its promise and its potential problems are out of reach. You can do nothing about tomorrow until it has arrived.

That leaves only today. Remember Christ's words on this?

"Don't worry at all then about tomorrow. Tomorrow can take care of itself! One day's trouble is enough for one day" (Matt. 6:34, Phillips).

Dr. William Osler, internationally known physician, once

35

wrote: "No man ever sank beneath the burden of the day. But if the load of tomorrow be added to that of yesterday and carried today, it will make the strongest falter."

But how can you keep from collecting more than a day's worth of fears?

"The secret," writes distinguished Christian counselor John S. Bonnell, "live in day-tight compartments, live one day at a time. Live today. That is all that God asks of any of us."

But worries are only surface indications of the deeper problem. They spring from the accumulated anxieties that we often harbor until they near the breaking point.

What can deal with the real causes deep inside us? Only some power stronger than even our fears. And of all the powers within us, fear is near the top. In second place, by most estimates. It's an unbelievably potent force. It can enslave millions, silence the concern of multitudes, beat into submission the hordes of average world citizens. Fear can be used to accomplish most ends and objectives.

But the greatest force of power in any man's life is not fear, but love. Love that is proven in a man's commitments, love that is shown in a man's loyalty, love that is demonstrated by a man's faith.

Love that is stronger even than fear.

The Bible says it perfectly:

Love contains no fear—indeed fully-developed love expels every particle of fear, for fear always contains some of the torture of feeling guilty. This means that the man who lives in fear has not yet had his love perfected. So have we come to know and trust the love God has for us. God is love, and the man whose life is lived in love does, in fact, live in God, and God does, in fact, live in him. So our love for him grows more and more, filling us with complete confidence for the day when he shall judge all men—for we realise that our life in this world is actually his life lived in us. (I John 4:18, 16, 17, Phillips).

36

That is the key to replacing fear—displace it with love. Love shoves out fear. Love crowds its way into control. When we admit the love of God into our lives by pledging to love Him—with heart, soul, strength and mind, He enters with the gift of His strength—to love.

Then God in return comes to be His loving self within us His healing touch resolves the anxieties of our hearts as we consciously surrender them to Him.

Then faith—faith means "loving obedience"—replaces fear. "The only known cure for fear is faith," writes Chicago psychiatrist Dr. William Sadler. Faith is the mood of the soul when a man has discovered that God loves him—and he can love God in return.

Then a sense of peace arises to quiet his heart. Peace is that sense of rightness, of restfulness, of relaxation that comes from a heart controlled and motivated by love rather than by fears.

We take a long stride in maturing—when we examine our fears to sort out the healthy, constructive fears from the useless, destructive anxieties.

We take a second step when we open our fear-choked selves to the forgiving, loving, healing touch of Christ.

We begin to realize the benefits of maturing when we let the love of God so permeate our lives that fear is squeezed out.

Can you get the best of your fears?

Yes, by God's help you can.

As the Bible pledges. . ."*For God has not given us a spirit of fear, but a spirit of power and love and a sound mind*" *(II Tim. 1:7, Phillips).*

CHAPTER SIX

Can You Do Your Best in Conversation?

Your words are you.

No, not completely, but to a far greater extent than you would dream possible.

Just as money is your time turned into exchangeable cash through work, so your words are your personality put in understandable, exchangeable form through speech.

In fact, personality is communication. To be able to enter into communication with other persons is personality.

Man is person inasmuch as he can speak, and inasmuch as one can speak to him and with him. The whole difference between an individual and a person is that the individual associates, whereas, the person communicates.[1]

So writes Swiss physician Dr. Paul Tournier in his book, *The Meaning of Persons.*

To be all you can be, as a constantly maturing person, you must draw the best from conversation. You must do your best in communication.

Certainly most of us do enough of it. If all the talking time of a lifetime were compressed into one continuous speech, the average person would spend thirteen years talking; that's 18,000 words a day, a book of 54 pages. In a year's time, that would add up to 66 books of 800 pages each, a twelve-foot shelf full. In a lifetime that shelf would stretch to three lengths of a football field.

A lot of words! What dreary reading it would make since we often do so much less than our best!

But how do we begin maturing in communication? First, by listening. Listening is the other half of talking, and in many ways the most important half. Loving is listening. Caring is hearing.

Love is the opening of your life to another. Through sensitive listening, sincere interest and simple attentive understanding. An open ear given to another is the only believable sign of an open heart.

To love your neighbor is to listen to him as you listen to yourself. The Golden Rule of friendship is — listen to others as you would have them listen to you.

The maturing person is first a listening person. He listens with his eyes, not letting them stray away and betray his wandering attention. He listens with his questions, not probing, interrogating, cross-examining or suggesting impatience or superiority. He listens with his answers, making sure they actually come in reply to what the other person has said.

He doesn't ignore the other's ideas, letting them fly by while he plans some sage word to use at the next opportunity for comment. Nor does he interrupt the other, or even worse, second-guess them by trying to read their thoughts, finish their sentence or supply the missing word when the other reaches for a forgotten phrase.

Instead he hears not only the words spoken, but the feelings expressed. He goes beyond the words and phrases to hear the ideas, the attitudes, the expressions of the real intent.

That is love for others put in action. Love is a warm listening ear. And that communicates far more than many words.

Haven't you experienced it? Have you never talked with someone who listened with such abandon and attention to what you were trying to say, that it drew the words and ideas from your heart? Called forth things you didn't know that you felt and knew? Even helped clarify your thoughts by the earnest quality of the other's listening?

Or has the reverse happened when you started out to vent your inner agonies and complain against your circumstances, but your friend's understanding love given in complete attention made you see things in a new light? And instead of collecting a quart of sweet sympathy, you simply unloaded your problem?

That's the power of listening love.

Nothing is more needed. Particularly by people with problems. . .and that includes almost all of us.

The Bible says, *"In view of what he has made us then, dear brothers, let every man be quick to listen but slow to use his tongue, and slow to lose his temper" (James 1:19, Phillips).*

Step one in doing your best in communication? Listening in love. Step two? Forgetting. Forgetting in love.

A major part of what you hear is no worth recalling. And an even greater part is not worth repeating. The maturing person learns to discard much of what he takes in from others. As he discovers that maturing minds discuss values, ideals and loving concerns; that stalled, static minds discuss events and happenings; and that childishly immature minds discuss only people and personalities in criticism and gossip, so he rejects and junks much of what he hears as useless for his own growth, pointless for friendship and dangerous to the victim, be he friend or enemy.

Would you like to check out your own ability to forget?

Can you forget a bit of damaging information about someone who stands in your way to success, or has even sabotaged your progress?

Can you forgo the privilege of passing on a bit of gossip about someone who has achieved the success you've missed, or gotten the wealth or fame you've wished for, or enjoyed that wealth by conspicuously consuming it in front of you?

Can you forgive the injuries another has done to you— just when you have the opportunity to strike back in conversation, wound the other with whip-words, or rub salt in the already open sores between you?

Why does gossip fascinate? Perhaps because it allows us to fulfill our worst inclinations by proxy.

And that can be true for both the gossiper and gossipee. It takes two to gossip. The receiver is just as guilty as the speaker. No maturing person can stand by while an absent and often innocent person is dirtied. It is our human responsibility to protest any possible smearing of a fellow human. Why not gently say, "I'd rather not listen to the criticism of another when he's not present to explain or to defend himself." Or ask, "Why do you think I should know this story about him or her?"

Gossip is no toy. It poisons the gossiper, prejudices the listener, and ambushes the victim. It leads to envy, anger, malice, suspicion, violence and murder. It obviously invalidates all personal claims to maturity.

The Bible says:

If any one appears to be "religious" but cannot control his tongue, he deceives himself and we may be sure that his religion is useless (James 1:26, Phillips).

And the Bible puts gossip alongside of lying, stealing, adultery, murder. It can be all of these in the heart and on the tongue. (See Col. 3:5-9, Rom. 1:24-32, Matt. 15:19.)

How well do you do in forgetting, forgoing, forgiving? The man who is maturing in conversation—in the gifts of communication learns such arts carefully, and practices them scrupulously.

As the Bible says:

For, dear brothers, you have been given freedom: not

freedom to do wrong, but freedom to love and serve each other. For the whole Law can be summed up in this one command: "Love others as you love yourself." But if instead of showing love among yourselves you are always critical and catty, watch out! Beware of ruining each other (Galatians 5:13,15, Living Letters).

A simple rule of immeasurable worth in maturing is. . . "Never pass on anything about anybody that will do any injury in any way."

From step one, listening—in love; and step two, forgetting—in love; we move to step three, speaking—in love.

Listening in order to understand the other person and forgetting in order to protect the other both combine to earn the right of speaking.

Speaking—in love—is the art of opening your life to another in self-disclosure. Of giving the other a clear insight into your self with its motives and meanings, and it is participation in the other person and personality.

It is here that a man's character and worth become obvious. His words communicate what he truly is as a person. And the maturing man's words, said Jesus, are oath-free and crystal clear. Listen:

". . .I say to you, don't use an oath at all. Whatever you have to say let your 'yes' be a plain 'yes' and your 'no' be a plain 'no'—anything more than this has a taint of evil" Matt. 5:33b, 37, Phillips).

Such conversation is—as St. Paul once wrote, as simple and clear as "yes" and "no." Check:

Do you think I plan with my tongue in my cheek, saying "yes" and meaning "no"? We solemnly assure you that as certainly as God is faithful so we have never given you a message meaning "yes" and "no" (II Cor. 1:17, 18, Phillips).

The maturing man does not need to spice his conversation with oaths in order to make it interesting, or brace it up with the gutsy language of the farmyard or shipyard. He is free—because of what he is—to speak simply, clearly, cleanly.

My fellow carpenter grimaced with sudden pain as his hammer glanced off a spike and onto a nail—his thumbnail. "Dammit," he said as he blew on his discolored thumb.

"Was that your first prayer of today?" I asked him.

"Prayer? That was no prayer," he replied. . .

"Wasn't it?" I asked. "Weren't you asking God for a little favor?"

"Well, maybe so," he said. . ."Well, I'll be d'. . .oh, I almost said it again." He chuckled, then continued, "That just goes to show how little it means."

"Then why swear?" I asked.

"That's just it. Why swear? Why do I swear anyway?" he asked in agreement.

What reasons are there for coloring conversation with additives?

Is it only to release frustration when under the stress of a deep emotion like anger, fear or shock?

Or is it a way to let off steam in any moment of pressure? To vent impatience or imitation immediately in words appropriate to the feelings?

The American Civil Liberties Union, in defending a man charged with "cussing out a cop" maintained in court that swearing is good for you. I quote: "Cursing relieves tension and provides an emotional safety valve against incidents which might lead to violence. . .swearing itself has no tendency to provoke violence."

Does it release frustration? Hardly. Instead of cooling anger, it excites it. Instead of reducing impatience, it multiplies it. Instead of indicating maturity, it refutes it. Instead of giving wider acceptance, it negates it. Instead of improving communication, it blocks it. Instead of reinforcing your ideas, it weakens them.

Then why swear? The real reasons aren't quite so obvious, are they? Could they be—one: Swearing is a compulsion caught from others and difficult to kick? Two: Swearing is a passion—a passion of anger, hostility or impatience—that is hard to lick? Three: Swearing is an expression of deeper hostility and irreverence against God Himself?

All of your deeper goals—to be respected, appreciated, listened to, understood—all these can be achieved best by clean, clear speech.

Swearing only cheapens, profanity actually destroys what you are trying to build. Isn't profanity just the effort of a feeble mind to express itself forcibly? With an unbelievable wealth of adjectives and adverbs at our disposal, why limit yourself to a few misused words of irreverent and irrelevant meaning. What an abuse of the gift of words!

The deeper tragedy is the hard fact that swearing is an absolute insult to the God of the universe. Many a polite, well-bred man who is gentle and understanding with his fellowmen slaps his Creator in the face daily in speech.

But the third of God's Ten Commandments still stands unbroken. . .in spite of our claims of breaking the law.

Thou shalt not take the name of the Lord thy God in vain, for the Lord will not hold him guiltless that taketh his name in vain. You shall not profane my holy name, but I will be hallowed among the people (Exodus 20:7, KJV; Lev. 22:32, RSV).

The maturing man—speaking in love—is truly at liberty to tell it like it actually is and be telling the truth. He has determined with the help of God to be the truth in all his relationships with others.

He can tell, do, and be the truth.

Truth is always consistent with itself. It doesn't need any help to stand alone. But a lie is always crippled. It needs a second lie for a brace. . .then another for a crutch. It's easy to tell a lie, but it's hard to tell only one lie.

But what is a lie? And what is lying?

Any untrue statement? No. . .let's say (1) any willfully untrue statement, (2) any deliberate false representation, (3) any intentional design to mislead or deceive, (4) any attempt to withhold information another rightfully and justly deserves to know.

The key to any and all definitions of lies and lying is—the intention—the motive—the attitude of the heart. Any intentional deception—even though it is said in words that are true in themselves—is a lie.

Like the lady, in the days of World War II sugar rationing who went to the ration board to request extra sugar stamps. "All the sugar we have in the house is what's on the kitchen table," she said plaintively. "How much sugar is on your kitchen table?" asked the official. "Two-hundred pounds," blurted the little boy by her side.

No matter how true a statement may be—it can be a deliberate lie in intention, and what is false in intent is false in fact. It's the motive that matters most.

It is not enough—it is never enough to simply talk of telling the truth. A man can tell the truth and be a liar still. All he has to do is select which truths to tell, or which half truths to combine and with a smattering of skill, and "with a little bit of luck" he can be an "honest" liar.

We all know too well how news can be "managed" to make it tell the story desired, or how events can be distorted to protect national or personal interests. And it can be done while sticking to the facts. True facts, of course, but carefully selected.

It is not enough to talk of telling the truth, or even of telling the whole truth.

You must be the truth. Be a true person. Be truly human. Be true to yourself, be true to others, and be true to God, the source of all truth.

Yes, it is important that you tell the truth and nothing but the truth to others. But you must face the real question, get down to the real issue. Ask yourself: "Am I willing to be the truth, to do the truth?"

It's one thing to say the truth—it's another to be it.

Most men say they love the truth, claim to tell the truth, and insist that they always want the truth. But are they willing to be true? To be the truth?

That's what makes Jesus Christ stand out from the billions. He said, *"I am the truth" (John 14:6).* Those nearest Him confirmed it. John writes: *"God became a human being and lived among us. We saw his splendour. . .full of grace and truth. . .for. . .love and truth came through Jesus Christ" (John 1:14,17, Phillips).*

And He asked us to be as true as the light, without any shadow of dishonesty in us.

What a release that is, to become a new, true person, to become the truth. And what a relief it is to be the truth. To be truly yourself before God, before others—and before yourself. No need to run and hide. No more games of hide-and seek with your conscience. No more faking. No more phony playacting. No more false fronts or faces.

That's when a man is free. Free to be the truth, the whole truth and nothing but the truth—by the help of God.

He can truly be himself in conversation with another. In communication with any other.

He can listen with love, releasing the other person to be himself in conversation.

He can forget in love, protecting the other person by burying anything he hears that may injure or destroy.

He can speak with love, sharing life in an open and interested way.

He can enter into relationships of understanding love for others. And this is maturing.

So it can be for you. Your words are you. Or so Jesus said. Remember?

". . .a man's words depend on what fills his heart. A good man gives out good—from the goodness stored in his heart; a bad man gives out evil—from his store of evil. I tell you that men will have to answer at the day of judgment for every careless word they utter—for it is your words that will acquit you, and your words that will condemn you" (Matt. 12:34-37, Phillips)!

47

Can it be that your words may be the perfect index to what you are?

Could it be that your words might be the perfect prophecy of what you are becoming?

What you want to be tomorrow, your conversation should be today. What you will be tomorrow, your words are showing today.

CHAPTER SEVEN

Can You Make the Most of What You Have?

Are you contented with life?

Have you ever been contented with your life?

My answer to those questions is "yes" and "no." What is yours?

Not that I'm torn by indecision like the man who complained to his doctor that he was never able to make up his mind on anything. "Would you like help on this problem?" the doctor asked. "Well, yes and no," he replied.

Contentment is a yes and no matter.

"No" to the contentment with what we are that cops out on moving toward maturity.

But "yes" to the contentment with what we have which frees us to become, to mature, to discover wholesome life.

Once a man arrives at a state of contentment with what he is, he's stalled, gone stale, stagnated. The man who is content with what he is or what he has done will never be or become his best. Once a man says, "I don't want to know any more, do any more, be any more," he's dead on his feet.

He has not arrived at maturity, he's a mummy. "No" to such self-contentment.

And "no" to the contentment that turns people into mere consumers.

Contentment is a warm sty for eaters and sleepers," playwright Eugene O'Neill once wrote rejecting the consumer style of life.

The eater-sleeper type of contentment is a satisfaction with purely material things. It breeds the viewpoint that the more we consume, the more others will respect us; so we consume as conspicuously as possible. The only discontent involved is in the drive to work harder to get more to be able to consume more conspicuously so that others will see us and supposedly admire us more and more. What a cycle!

If this is our contented conclusion, then nothing can halt our turning into one continental pigsty where nothing can persuade us to lift our snouts from the trough.

No—a thousand noes to such contentment.

But "yes" to the contentment that frees a man from the clamor of drives and desires that make him a slave to things, to possessions, to potential fame. "Yes" to the contentment that frees him from being the servant of his own appetites and ambitions. "Yes" to the contentment that lets him be at peace with himself in the face of the external pressures of consumerism and statis-itis so that he can get on with the real business of living, growing and maturing.

"Yes" to the contentment that breaks a man loose from an obsession with influence. Power is a psychedelic drug that blows a man's sanity in relation to others. But the freedom of maturing contentment can release him from the worship of fame—power through popularity or prestige, or from the exercise of economic power, institutional power, executive power, political power or any of the other power positions that turn men into creatures who exploit others.

"Yes" to the contentment that cuts a man loose from any obsession with affluence and the false power that it brings.

This is the point where a man is most vulnerable to a destructive discontent.

Wealth can be an uncontrollable obsession. An almost inescapable addiction. It gains an unconscious hold on a man and its grip grows and grows until at last he's under the influence.

The influence of affluence.

Money. Pure 200-proof money. Taken straight or mixed with many lovely things, is the most intoxicating substance known to man. The most habit-forming. The most incurable addiction is money-loving.

And there are pushers everywhere you turn. It takes no ABC license to promote the luxury habit. Anyone can be a money-fever junkie. Anyone can and will influence others to come under the influence of affluence.

And it shows up in such subtle ways. The way an affluence-addict's eyes light up at the sight of new products, new lines of merchandise, new luxury items. (Ever see such thirst?)

Or the way he drives himself to afford or acquire anything that catches his fancy. (Ever see such addiction?) Or the way she may play the big-spender role. (Ever go on such a bender?) Or the way a family will sacrifice time, leisure, relationship, and each other to get all the things they want now and hate later. (What a way to be a wealth-a-holic!)

You know people like that—the Joneses next door; you know, the ones who are always getting ahead.

What are the symptoms that affluence may be bringing you under its influence? The same as any other intoxication.

A surface sense of exhilarating pleasure.

A false feeling of security.

An insatiable, burning thirst for more and ever more.

A slow insensitivity to the needs of others maturing to a final state of total oblivion to all but yourself.

A death to concern, compassion, and communication with both God and man.

How can this be?

Like any intoxication, the first flush of wealth may bring an illusion of exhilaration, of accelerated pleasures. It may inebriate a man with the gentle blush of success, giving him a false sense of well-being. As he gradually slips under the influence, the comfort and safety of wealth deadens insight and depresses his perspective on reality producing a near-sighted security all out of proportion with things as they are. A love of money and its powers, a trust in things and their abilities can desensitize a man to anything beyond the moment and its enjoyment.

As a man slips into the deeper intoxication abundance and affluence causes, his appreciation of himself tends to grow. Slowly his personal estimate of his own worth and importance slips beyond the level of believability. He may become boasting-bragging drunk-priding himself in dollar-sign values of his own worth.

Or it may be a more subtle change of personal values. A man begins contrasting what he has with those beneath him to nourish his pride. At the same time, he can't help comparing what he does not have with the affluence of those above him to feed his envy.

All of this fires an insatiable hunger for more, a thirst for greater, better, larger, richer things. Wealth becomes master. Wealth-a-holism is only a grand or two away. And they wealthy themselves to death.

For example:

The enterprise of a certain businessman brought high returns. And he thought to himself, "How shall I exploit my advantage to the full? This I will do. I shall double my holdings in the corporation, the stock will rise and I shall be secure forever!" But that night he had a coronary.

Again:

The investments of a certain banker began to rise on the stock market. And he said to himself, "How can I convert my finances into a fortune? This I will do. I will invest more shrewdly, my stocks will compound, divide and double, and I shall have wealth beyond my wildest dreams of pleasure." But that night he had a stroke.

Or, as Jesus told the story in its original words:

"Once upon a time a rich man's farmland produced heavy crops. So he said to himself, 'What shall I do, for I have no room to store this harvest of mine?' Then he said, 'I know what I'll do. I'll pull down my barns and build bigger ones where I can store all my grain and my goods and I can say to my soul, Soul, you have plenty of good things stored up there for years to come. Relax! Eat, drink and have a good time!' But God said to him, 'You fool, this very night you will be asked for your soul! Then, who is going to possess all that you have prepared?' That is what happens to the man who hoards things for himself and is not rich where God is concerned" (Luke 12:16b-21, Phillips).

The tragic end of a wealth-a-holic.

But many men die the slow death of creeping lethargy, apathy, and indifference that affluence brings the man who loves prosperity and its pleasures.

Affluence is the perfect anesthesia for helping a man forget the pain of others. It anesthetizes conscience, compassion, and common concern. At first you may still feel a touch of sympathy or pity, but it soon goes away. A few forgotten good intentions that never mature to actions insure our permanent inactivity. At last it isolates a man with his money-mania, cutting him off from both God and man.

Small wonder the Word we have from God demands a complete liberty from affluence-addiction.

We brought absolutely nothing with us when we entered this world and we can be sure we shall take absolutely nothing with us when we leave it. . .For men who set their hearts on being wealthy expose themselves to temptation . . .For loving money leads to all kinds of evil, and some men in the struggle to be rich have lost their faith and caused themselves untold agonies of mind. . .Set your heart not on riches, but on goodness, Christ-likeness, faith, love, patience and humility. . .Tell those who are rich in this present world not to be contemptuous of others, and not to rest the weight of their confidence on the transitory power of wealth but on the living God, who generously gives us everything for our enjoyment. Their security should be invested in the life to come, so that they may be sure of holding a share in the life which is permanent (I Tim. 6:7, 9-11, 17, 19, Phillips).

Now, may we get right down to cases. . .your case and mine? Are we so sure we haven't been slipping under the influence of affluence? What kind of hold on your life do your possessions have?

Check.

Do you just *like* a little money? When you get it, have it, use it, you feel happier, better, more secure than you actually are?

Do you ever notice that you're not as interested in meeting the meaningful expenses of life as you are in the money left over for use after your obligations are met?

Do you catch yourself evaluating your work only by the size of the salary, not by the rewards of the service rendered?

Do you think you would compromise your principles, or sacrifice an opportunity to be of greater service for others, just to take a job offering more money?

Do you work such long hours and invest so much of your energy to money-making that you sacrifice your wife, your children, your own spiritual and mental health in the process?

Do you find your money-making business crowding into your mind at most times—at play, at home, at worship, at times of service to others?

Do you tend to value all time given to your family, your church, your neighbors in terms of what you could have made if you had been working instead?

Do you ever find yourself measuring your happiness

in terms of your possessions, your property, your prestige?

Or try this test suggested by Albert Day in *Discipline and Discovery:*

The proof of our thing-mindedness is again, very easy. Try for five minutes to give God the loving attention, which is the essence of true prayer. You will find your mind reverting over and over to things—to what you are wearing or what you would like to wear, to what you had for breakfast or what you want for lunch, to the salary you receive or the increase you are seeking, to the house you live in or the house you are trying to find, to the condition of your car or the prospect of a new one! With amazing frequency things in some fashion will insert themselves into your brief effort to keep your mind fixed on God.[1]

So...how can you break the strangle hold of things, wealth, and affluence?

First: Let God be God—of your life and your wealth.

Jesus said:

"No one can be loyal to two masters. He is bound to hate one and love the other, or support one and despise the other. You cannot serve God and the power of money at the same time." (Matt. 6:24, Phillips).

Second: Let things be things—use them to serve man and God. Never let them master your loyalties or order your priorities.

The Bible says:

Never give your hearts to this world or to any of the things in it. A man cannot love the Father and love the world at the same time (I John 2:15, Phillips).

How is this done?

It is done by putting personal values and persons above material values and things.

Most of our human discontent is expended over things. Things we want, but can't have. So we end up being jealous of those who do have them and enjoy them in front of us. Things we reach for but can't get. So we turn up using people like pawns, and abusing other people like things in an effort to get any way getting is possible. Things we fight for but can't reach. So we wind up hating ourselves and others because we have failed or fallen by the way.

But the contentment which values people first and things second lets us accept life as we have found it and be our best with what we have. It is happiness.

Remember how Jesus said:

"How happy are the humble-minded, for the kingdom of Heaven is theirs!

"Happy are those who claim nothing, for the whole earth will belong to them!

"Happy are those who are hungry and thirsty for goodness, for they will be fully satisfied" (Matt. 5:3, 5, 6; Phillips)!

"So don't worry and don't keep saying, 'What shall we eat, what shall we drink or what shall we wear?'! That is what pagans are always looking for; your Heavenly Father knows that you need them all. Set your heart on his kingdom and his goodness, and all these things will come to you as a matter of course" (Matt. 6:31-33, Phillips).

Second, this contentment is made by placing eternal values ahead of momentary, temporary matters.

When a man lives only for the moment, he has no perspective. When he lives only for the instant pleasure of his situation, he's always "under the circumstances."

But once he discovers how to find the peace of contentment in long-term goals, in values that are beyond himself, in purposes that are eternal, he can live "above the circumstances." He can live "beyond his means"; not financially, but emotionally and spiritually.

St. Paul is a perfect example of such contentment. Never satisfied with himself and his own levels of maturity, he could say in discontent:

How changed are my ambitions! Yet, my brothers, I do not consider myself to have "arrived", spiritually, nor do

I consider myself already perfect. But I keep going on, grasping ever more firmly that purpose for which Christ Jesus grasped me.

All of us who are spiritually adult should set ourselves this sort of ambition (Phil. 3:10a, 12, 15a, Phillips).

And then, a few breaths later he could express his complete contentment, saying:

I have learned to be content, whatever the circumstances may be. I know now how to live when things are difficult and I know how to live when things are prosperous. In general and in particular I have learned the secret of facing either plenty or poverty. I am ready for anything through the strength of the one who lives within me (Phil. 4:11b, 12, 13; Phillips).

That's the sort of contentment that marks a maturing man. He's making the most of what he has in order to be all that he can become.

Is self-sufficiency the secret? No. If there is a secret, it is discovering and releasing the strength of Christ within.

The man who truly knows Christ, loves Christ, and follows Christ daily in his style of life has an inner strength that can cope with anything.

He is no longer pushed all out of shape by external pressures, nor is he uptight over inner ambitions or appetites.

He is free to live at his constantly maturing best. He has the contentment of peace. The contented peace which Christ gives.

So he accepts himself, his own gifts and talents, his own inabilities and areas of weakness. He accepts his situation in life, his own possessions, his position or lack of the same.

So he sets his true values. People are more important than things. Life is more significant than wealth. Emotional-spiritual maturity is more valuable than prosperity.

And he does his best with what is given him. Making the most of what he has in creative pursuit of the way of Christ, not in conflict with values Jesus lived.

Content with what we are? Yes, we're using it as a means of becoming better persons in the maturity of Christ's style of life.

Content with what we are? No, we're only beginning to be all we can be through the strength of Jesus.

CHAPTER EIGHT

Can You Be Your Best in Failure?

The class prophecy had just been opened at a ten-year high school class reunion, the roll had been called and all accounted for but one.

"Read his prophecy first," someone suggested.

"George A. Jones, unanimously voted 'least-likely-to-succeed,' will be driver-second-class for the greater Hoboken garbage disposal company."

As the laughter that followed subsided, a chauffeur-driven limousine pulled to the curb outside, a gentleman was assisted to the curb. He was impeccably attired from the imported Irish tweeds to the shoes of oiled alligator. It was Jones, of course.

When the silence that greeted his arrival had broken again into conversation, an old friend sidled up.

"How'd you achieve all the success?" he asked.

"Well," Jones replied, "I got into the business of handling potatoes. Buy 'em for a dollar a bag, sell 'em for two. And you know, that one percent profit adds up faster than you'd suppose."

Whatever the reasons given for any man's success, it is obviously as impossible to predict as it is to evaluate. Who knows who will succeed? Who can say who has truly succeeded?

Take this man's credentials for analysis:

If his teacher told him that he was an idiot.

If his employer told him that he was stupid.

If his mother-in-law told him that her daughter should have married a doctor.

If he lost his previous job.

If nobody loves him.

If he doesn't know where he's going in life.

If he wouldn't give you two cents for his future.

He's not a born loser.

He is the ideal insurance salesman for a nationally prominent life-insurance firm. They promise to make him a certain success by becoming to him. . .

. . .the teacher who loved him,

. . .the mother-in-law who thinks he's great,

   .the coach who gave him nine letters in athletics.

. . .the boss who wants to make him president.

That's security. "From the minute we hire a man," they promise, "he is in our house for the rest of his life. He, his wife, his children, his dreams become our responsibility. There is no firing in this company. A man has to be a thief to be fired."[1]

In spite of such guarantees, even financial success is never absolutely certain in life. In life—what is?

And when you step over to evaluate a man's total impact as a person—who can evaluate, promise or predict?

Success is never certain!

Even if you should succeed in life, you'll never know it!

Yes, you read me right. You will never be sure of success, no matter how well you meet your goals.

How can anyone measure the impact, the contribution,

the success of a life?

A case in point: the life of a young man from the Midwest.

He began at 22 as a partner in a crossroads store, investing seven years' savings and finding sudden failure punctuated by a sheriff's sign on the door.

After two years of struggle to accumulate another stake, he tries again. But his new partner drinks up the profits, an associate takes French leave with all cash on hand and the young man is left to shoulder the liability for both; fifteen years would pass before he had paid his way out of debt.

He makes a try as a surveyor, but a creditor attached his instruments and horse.

Then his fiancee dies, grief and depression overwhelm him and his health and sanity break down tragically. "At this period of my life I never dared to carry a pocketknife," he wrote long afterward.

Ten years later, some of his friends nudged him into politics and secured his election to Congress, but he lost his bid for re-election.

Nine years later he tried for the Senate, failing at the last minutes. Two years later he failed again disastrously.

Two more years pass, and then Abraham Lincoln was elected President of the United States. And then again four years later only to be defeated finally by an assassin's derringer.

A tragic life. One failure following another. Yet, he is honored as one of his nation's greatest successes.

Success or failure—who is sufficient to judge? Who knows what constitutes failure or success for any man?

Does a life of successive failures crowned by one final triumph equal success?

Or can a life of achievement fade tó failure just because of a last defeat? All because of the events of one tragic hour?

Our measurements are all too subjective, too biased. For example. There was a big league baseball player who struck out a record 1,330 times. A failure? No, he also hit a record 714 home runs. His name? Babe Ruth.

True success cannot be measured either accurately or honestly.

Certainly not by the popular earmarks of success — wealth, position, fame, reputation, influence and all that.

Obviously not by all the ideas of popular propaganda that persuade us to buy this, try that, join this, conform to that and instant success will crown you. Nonsense.

Yes, you may be able to gauge your progress through life by reaching short-term goals. Of course you may be able to achieve a succession of small successes in your work, your group, your community.

But in terms of a life, in the perspective of a lifetime, what is success? What yardsticks can you use?

In his book, *Letters to My Sons,* author Dogabert Runes writes, "The true measure of success in life lies in production for the use and the welfare of the community. And of all failings, the ugliest is the lust for personal success."

That's using the yardstick of "How much have you contributed to the community?" Very difficult to measure.

A second measuring stick for success. For multimillionaire Henry Ford, who said, "Success? Success is to do more for the world than the world does for you."

But who can claim that. Every one of us is indebted to so many persons that evaluation is impossible.

Albert Einstein, one of the greatest mathematical minds of the twentieth century wrote on this:

"A successful man is he who receives a great deal from his fellowmen, usually incomparably more than corresponds to his service to them. The value of a man, however, should be seen in what he gives and not in what he is able to receive.[2]

Ralph Waldo Emerson once gave a beautiful definition for success that carries us one step farther:

To laugh often and much;

To win the respect of intelligent people,
  And the affection of children;
To earn the appreciation of honest critics
  And endure the betrayal of false friends;
To appreciate beauty;
To find the best in others;
To leave the world a bit better,
  Whether by a healthy child
    a garden patch
      or a redeemed social condition;
To know even one life has breathed easier because you
  lived.[3]
This is to have succeeded.

That's a much simpler bench mark. "Have you served?"
"Do you know how to serve?" "Do you find happiness
happening to you when you are serving others?"

Then you have reached success.

Service is success? Certainly service is one of life's highest
moments of meaning. Absolutely, service is the way to fulfillment and satisfaction.

But as a ruler it won't serve well at all. Service is not a
thing to be measured, it is a loving deed given self-forget-
fully. And how could you know whether your service made
better men of your fellows—or lazier men? Nobler men or
weaker, more parasitic people? When you sit at the other
end of life and look back with the 20-20-vision of hindsight,
how can you measure your success on the basis of service?
Impossible!

Service is a way of life, not a success to be achieved, as
the late Dr. Albert Schweitzer wisely pointed out. A
theologian, author, artist, teacher, he left it all to study
medicine and become a doctor in a primitive area of Africa.

"I don't know what your destiny will be," he once wrote,
"but one thing I know. The only ones among you who will
be really happy are those who will have sought and found
how to serve."

How then can we measure our success?

We can't. Unless we are materialists, gauging our progress by possessions, public acclaim or apparent prestige.

But once you choose to live by inner goals, once your supreme values are those of the Spirit—values like love, acceptance, forgiveness, truthfulness, wholeness and holiness—then measurement is obsolete. Useless. Irrelevant.

Ultimately, we cannot and will not know whether we have succeeded.

God knows and God alone can judge.

He does not hold us responsible for success, He holds us responsible for obedience.

He does not demand that we accomplish great things, but that we attempt them.

I am absolutely convinced that Jesus Christ has called those of us who seek to follow Him daily in life. . .

To let every man, woman, and child on earth hear the Good News of life everlasting.

To let the whole world see His kind of living-by-love every day.

To help stop hunger, poverty, starvation and deprivation.

To end violence and war by calling men to a higher way of resolving conflict—Christ's way of understanding, repentance, and forgiveness.

To end prejudice, racism, and discrimination of whatever sort and style.

The list could go on. . .and on.

I'm committed to these things, with my whole heart. I've invested my life in their pursuit.

"But wait," you may ask, "do you honestly expect to evangelize the whole world, to end all war, to stamp out poverty and hunger, to silence prejudice, to bring in the kingdom of God?"

That question means nothing to me. It's a "success question." A non-question. I haven't been called to succeed in any of these things. Only to die trying.

I'll work with all my heart to bring in the kingdom of God. Whether we succeed or not is unimportant. It's the greatest life in the world, trying.

It's not the success that matters. It's faithfulness. To Jesus Christ.

It's not the measurable results that I live for, it's obedience to the way of Christ that matters supremely.

Christ calls us to be faithful, promises that our acceptance with God is not on the basis of performance—but of faithfulness. "Well done, thou good and faithful servant," He will say, "Come and share your Master's rejoicing." (See Matthew 25:19-23.)

Success — no. Faithful service — yes.

Listen again to Christ's words:

"You know that the so-called rulers in the heathen world lord it over them, and their great men have absolute power. But it must not be so among you. No, whoever among you wants to be great must become the servant of you all, and if he wants to be first among you he must be the slave of all men! For the Son of Man himself has not come to be served but to serve, and to give his life to set many others free" (Mark 10:42b-45, Phillips).

The whole point is loving, obedient, faithful service to God and to your fellow humans.

Not success. Faithful service.

Just look at Jesus. The cross looked like dismal failure. It turned out to be the triumph of all history. Christ's way of defenseless suffering love looks like madness in an evil world, and yet. . .it's the way of Christ.

It guarantees no success, not even survival.

But it's God's way. The way of loving truth.

So, who knows if we shall succeed or fail in life? Who cares? Following Christ offers us perfect freedom to fail. Knowing that God accepts us in spite of our failures, we don't need to hide them, or even fear them. We can admit and accept failure. In following Christ, we're free to fail. He never promised us that we would always be safe, be right, be successful.

He only promised us freedom, meaning, and joy. Forever.

Our part? Faithfulness.

Our goal? Faithfulness.

Not success. Faithfulness.

CHAPTER NINE

Can You Make the Most of Your Sexuality?

To the eager reader who turned to this chapter first, I must quickly say, this is not primarily a discussion of making the most of sex—important as that may be—but of sexuality.

Not that I want to disappoint you. True, few topics can compete with the fascination of sexual matters. But there is a topic of almost equal interest and of even broader importance. It's sexuality.

Sexuality means understanding what it means to be man and woman in all of life.

Sexuality means understanding ourselves as sexual beings not only when we experience sexual desires, but in everything we do as a male or female person.

Sexuality has an every-day-ness and an any-place-ness that affects all our relationships, viewpoints, roles of service and opportunities for fulfillment in every area of life.

We are born as creatures of diffuse sexuality, and this un-directed force must be discovered, understood and directed to creative ends if we are to grow toward maturity. To be all you can be as a person—man type or woman type—requires a growing insight into your own sexuality and the freedom to fulfill it responsibly.

Can you be your best in sexuality? No sooner is that question asked than the questioner feels a need to shore himself up with explanations. Because most people read only the first three letters to any word beginning with S-E-X. Why this obsession?

A quick survey of the sex-scape of the seventies indicates. . .

Many men consider the sex drive as the most vital mainspring of human growth, development and behavior.

Many people assume that fullest satisfaction of sexual desires will produce health, happiness and emotional maturity.

Many persons view sexual inhibitions as the main source of emotional frustrations, mental illnesses, physical sicknesses and social criminality.

And none of these has been—nor can be—proven. Yet these assumptions are used to ridicule chastity, scoff at fidelity and glamorize sexual adventurism.

Where once upon a time man considered himself to be created in the image of God, now his self image is of a sexual creature powered by sexual drives and instincts, preoccupied with sexual dreams and fantasies, and measuring his own worth by his ability to attract, conquer and give satisfaction to members of the opposite sexual composition.

Certainly both sex and sexuality are involved in every part of life. But to say they control it all is nonsense. To say there is sexual influence in everything may be true. But to say sex is everything, or its influence determines everything is ridiculous.

What is our viewpoint as we move toward maturity in sexuality?

First, we respect our sexuality as a gift of God. Male and female we are created to end our aloneness through complementary union. To be man—or to be woman—is to be equally a part of the image of God. (Examine Genesis 1:27.) Since sexuality is in itself good, as all of God's creative works were, then we need not be ashamed or embarrassed that we happen to live in bodies.

Second, we accept our bodies as the handiwork of God. Not evil in themselves, but good. Bodies are good, you would never want to be without one. Bodies are respectable. Some of the best Christians I know have bodies. Bodies are useful. It's the only low-cost housing made by unskilled labor that progress can't improve. When God entered our world, He wasn't embarrassed to do it in a body. What was good enough for Him should be good enough for us. When Christ lived, taught, died and rose to life again, He did it in a body. We can respect the body and its sexuality. He did, and does.

Third, we can respect our sexual roles as men and women. We have no need to be ashamed of our sexuality in personality. Believe it! You are not a neutral human. You are a male human or a female human. One of two parts to the two-piece interlocking human puzzle. You are not complete in yourself. You are constructed to be complete only in union, communion and relation to another.

As the Original Designer said on the day man and woman were created; and as Jesus Christ said in clarifying the true purpose:

". . .the one who created them from the beginning made them male and female and said: 'For this cause shall a man leave his father and mother, and shall cleave to his wife; and the twain shall become one flesh' " (Matt. 19: 4b, 5, Phillips).

Male and female are created unique, uniquely dependent, uniquely dependent in a complementary relationship to each other. The goal is that male and female in a permanent, interdependent union should each complete the other.

What is more, there is a magnificently exuberant simplicity in these creation words.

As man cleaves to woman, she becomes his wife. She is not a thing, not a possession, not a sexual object for his pleasure, not a physical conquest for his masculine sexual prowess. She is woman. She is wife. She is a person. And the exuberance is shown in the joyous cleaving of man to woman as they become one flesh, bound together heart and life in a union never meant to be dissolved. That is a true picture of human sexuality as it was designed for maturing men and women.

The maturing person rejects the false ideas of what it means to be a sexual being in today's world, not because they are too sexual, but because they are not sexual at all.

Any ideas of sexuality that dehumanize one or both of the persons involved, any use or abuse of one another, any manipulation or exploitation is actually anti-sexual.

Any approach to sex as an activity apart from love, as a pleasure apart from the joy of unconditional relationship, as a physical release apart from the blending of two lives in total commitment is not sexual, mutual, nor authentic.

Maturing in sexuality begins as the person accepts responsibility for what he truly is before God and before his fellow humans.

Maturing in sexuality grows as we recognize the sexual dimensions of all our relationships with others and seek to fulfill them in the motivation of love-for-neighbor that seeks the best for others in all relationships.

Maturing advances as we seriously commit ourselves to God's particular concerns, limitations and directions for the expression of our sexuality. Explicitly, this means honoring His limitations that sexuality be expressed in physical union only when a truly spiritual, emotional and social union called marriage has first been established.

Maturing achieves liberty when our sexuality becomes a living response to self-giving love. To truly love means to respond to another in voluntary freedom. When God's love controls our total lives, the spontaneity of our relationships reflects His joy in us.

Maturing brings peace as we affirm that God forgives even our sexual mistakes and misuses, frees us from lust and twists of selfishness and frees us to love more as He loves in self-forgetful self-giving.

Maturing brings release as we let the strength of Christ's Spirit reinforce our controls, guide our motives and prompt our decision-making. He is our Maker. He services His products.

With these steps, you're becoming. Becoming mature. Becoming all you can be—physically, emotionally, spiritually, and in sexuality.

CHAPTER TEN

Can You Be Your Best in Marriage?

This is the crucial question in marital happiness.

Not—"Have you found the best partner possible?"

But—"Are you willing to be the best partner possible?"

A strange story is told about Biship Bompas, the first Anglican churchman to venture among the Indians of the Yukon. Discovering that none of the tribe had been baptized or married, he proceeded without further ado to do both. After the mass, five-hour baptismal and marriage ceremony was ended, he asked the chief which part the people enjoyed most.

"Well, Bishop," said the chief, "we like being baptized, but best of all we loved being married."

Suspicious, the Bishop asked, "Why did you prefer the marriage ceremony?"

"Because we all got new wives," said the chief.

There are a lot of red-faced people who belong to that same tribe, and long for a change of mate. But there are many more who'd just like to make a few changes in their mates, a few changes, they are quite sure, for the better.

If you could remold your husband's or wife's personality, or rearrange his or her value system. . .what would you change?

Once you begin making a list, where would you stop? But once you decide to carry it out, where would you start?

There's nothing that we human beings resist much more than change—except when it's our own idea. And when someone tries to change us—no matter who it is—it's threatening, and therefore, irritating.

Most of us are willing enough to be a helper-type person, but who of us wants to be helped? If you offer free lessons on how to be a helper, your class will pack the room. But just offer a course on how to be helped. No one. Why? To be helped means to be changed. And that is a threat to our private soul!

No wonder we all recoil from the person who wants to change us, even though we love them. Somehow, it's like the other person wants to recreate us into his own image and likeness. When that suspicion hits us, usually we can think of sixty-four undesirable traits in the person criticizing that justifies rejecting him with a "who is he to try to change me? Let him sweep his own doorstep first." (If even Jesus Christ had it thrown up to Him, "Physician, heal yourself;; (Luke 4:23), can you expect any better?)

But in spite of the difficulty it is possible to reform, to remake your husband or wife, if you know where to begin, how to proceed, and what to change.

Where shall you begin?

With yourself. Begin with you. Before you can have any hope of changing your partner, you will need to make some very crucial changes.

Since criticizing and suggesting changes only increase resistance—consciously or unconsciously—and since prodding and pushing only increase the problem by decreasing understanding, love and acceptance between you, discard it.

Stop it all. Determine to give the most wholehearted love and acceptance possible. Without conditions.

But then, if you can't criticize and correct the other, how will you proceed?

By being a different sort of person. Instead of accepting with spoken or unspoken reservations, genuinely accept him or her as you promised in that long ago ceremony. Vows are nothing if they do not become a way of life. A daily commitment of life. And your vows were not to educate, reform and restructure your mate, but to love.

The crucial commitment of marriage is the pledge to be the right mate to the other person. Forget whether you "found the right mate." Who could know? Who could say? And so what if you did or didn't discover just-the-very-very-right-and-perfect-person-for-grand-old-you.

What kind of person are you being? Are you committed to being the right mate here and now? Do that, be that, and you'll make a change for the better in both of you. Almost instantly.

The mature husband is the man who says, "I have chosen a wife. From this day on I will not look for someone who might please me more and suit me better, but I will look for ways to be more pleasing and better suited to the one I have chosen."

You see, the belief that each of us is absolutely entitled to *receive* happiness from the marriage partner is at the bottom of most of our marriage troubles. We are not entitled to any such thing! What we do have is the privilege and the right of giving happiness to the other person. Once you discover how to accomplish that, you delightfully discover that you can hardly give happiness without getting it back in the process. Happiness happens to you as you are providing it to the other person, but never when you are demanding it for yourself.

When one person begins planning, loving, and living for the other a great step toward change in both persons has been made. In spite of all our clever concealing, it's perfectly obvious to a husband or wife whether the other's attention is really focused on his or her interest, or on your interest. Self-centeredness cannot be hidden. You know whether he or she is secretly hoping to reshape your life until it matches up to his or her own self-designed image of what you ought to be. And all of us both resent and resist such attempted changes.

The first help we can actually give each other is acceptance. Genuine acceptance. Mutual acceptance, as between equals.

"Acceptance in marriage is the power to love someone and receive him in the very moment that we realize how far he falls short of our hopes. Acceptance in marriage is love among equals," writes Gibson Winter in his book, *Love and Conflict*. "It is love between two people who see clearly that they do not measure up to one another's dreams. Acceptance is loving the real person to whom one is married. Acceptance is giving up dreams for reality."[1]

The second great help we must be willing to extend is genuine openness in communication.

If you see a couple sitting in a restaurant, in the park, or anywhere in public, watch their conversation.

If the woman is obviously impressed by each word the man murmurs, if he in turn eagerly awaits and welcomes her response, you can take it as a fact—unmarried.

But if she gazes absently in one direction, he stares another; when one's lips move and the other gives little or no indication of hearing, don't bother looking for a wedding ring. They couldn't be more married!

Oh yes, there are exceptions. Those few couples who cultivate the fine art of communication. Those few who are aware that marriage is a lifetime relationship dependent upon communication. Those couples who discover the secrets of communication in every relationship of marriage.

Strange, isn't it, that a couple falls in love by communication, nourishes it with their own unique codes of communication, and unites it in the spiritual, emotional, and physical communication of marriage—then suddenly they become speechless! Suddenly they can't—or don't—get through to each other anymore!

Not that they lose the ability: it's the desire to communicate that undergoes change.

In his book, *The Ways of Friendship,* psychiatrist Ignace Lepp writes: "The majority of conjugal misunderstanding that I have encountered professionally were not due to sexual incompatibility but to an almost total lack of communication of minds. Sexual incompatibility itself. . .is more frequently than not the result of a lack of spiritual communication."[2]

Of course, if communication could just cease when we stop talking, as we imagine it does, we could pick up our conversations where we left off. But communication never ends. Silence shouts. Avoidance betrays us. Withdrawal has a loud language of its own.

In marriage, we cannot stop communicating. In fact, we cannot NOT communicate. Because marriage is initiated by, pledged by, nourished by and totally dependent upon communication.

Can you see why communication is the skill most needed, most important, most crucial to the success of your marriage? If you are to be more than two associated people, if you are to be persons, truly human, truly alive, truly understanding each other, it must happen through wholesome communication.

What is this communication?

It is both giving and receiving. Speaking and listening. Or, stated accurately, it is both revelation of one's self, and participation in the other person.

It is not a matter of *how much* you talk to each other, but of *how* you talk to each other. Is your conversation carefully guarded or tactful and cautious? Does it skirt tender areas on all sides, avoiding the no-man's land which is unmarked but clearly recognized by both? Or does it freely reveal the real you in a natural, self-giving flow of revelation?

Revelation? Yes, true communication between husband and wife is self-disclosure. Self-revelation.

Love is the opening of yourself to another. It is sharing on the deeper levels of honesty and spiritual intimacy. Masks must drop, defenses fall. As we drop our guard, and look at each other unafraid, we begin the kind of communication that makes married love grow and mature.

Psychologist Erich Fomm expressed this well in his book, *The Art of Loving:*

Love is possible only if two persons communicate with each other from the center of their existence. . .Love experienced thus, is a constant challenge; it is not a resting place, but a moving, growing, working together. . .There is only one proof for the presence of love: the depth of the relationship, and the aliveness and strength in each person concerned; this is the fruit by which love is recognized.[3]

Such sharing "from the center of existence" is both verbal and nonverbal. Although it must first be expressed in speech if it is to be felt in silence. We often say that silence is more eloquent than speech, but this is only true when the silence is charged with the words exchanged before.

More often silence is not eloquent; it's an irritant. Like the wife who says to the husband hidden in his paper, "I think you should talk to me while I sew." To which he replies, "Why don't you sew to me while I read?"

But when a genuine openness for the flow of communication, both verbal and nonverbal exists, then a blending of lives, a complementary union takes place.

And acceptance grows. The unconditional acceptance that brings a marriage toward the discovery of all that life together can be. Change becomes a by-product as it should be. Adjustment each to the other is an incidental thing enroute to deeper understanding.

"All right," a husband may say, "so now you've said it. I can't change my wife. I've got to accept the way she is as reality, and resign myself."

Yes, that's right. You can't change your wife. That is, *you* can't. Only God made, makes and remakes people with the inner strength of love which He supplies. The change, if it comes, must come from within a person. From that strange inner spring of motivation called the will.

But a change can happen in you. And through you, a change will happen in your marriage. And because of you, a change may happen in her.

But such a change will only come as she sees how changed you are, and, because of your unconditioned acceptance and love, she too begins to want that same thing.

Who of us is ever pushed into change? We may be forced to modify our actions or pattern of life by some crisis in life or marriage, and we adjust out of necessity. But that is not truly change.

We are truly changed only when we are attracted and convinced by insights and understandings which bring a genuine change of heart. And we are changed in the deepest sense, only by the action of the Spirit of God within our lives.

Do you want to change your husband or wife? Then begin being the kind of changed person, in every way you know, that you would like him or her to become.

And the best blueprint known for being a genuinely changed partner-in-marriage is found in the Bible. Listen to St. Paul's words:

Wife...
Commit yourself
To your husband,
As you submit yourself
To the Lord Christ.

With the same love,
With the identical gentleness
That Christians show
In loyalty to their Master.
Respect your husband
With the same respect
You give to yourself.

Husband. . .
Give your wife
The same sort of love
That Christ gave to us
When he sacrificed himself for us.
Christ gave himself to change us
To make us holy, clean, right,
To make us altogether glorious in his eyes.
To free us from faults, blemishes or any other disfigure-
*   ment.*
So we men must give our wives
The same quality of love
We naturally have for ourselves, for our own bodies.
The love a man gives his wife
Is the extending of his love for himself to enfold her.
In practice what I have said amounts to this:
Let everyone of you who is a husband
Love his wife as he loves himself (Eph. 5:22-28, 33;
author's paraphrase).

To change another, change only yourself.

Give yourself. Without condition, without reservation. Christlike. Self-sacrificial. Self-forgetful.

Give yourself. Understandingly, sympathetically, acceptingly, acceptingly, acceptingly. . .

This is love. The most powerful, irresistible, life-changing force known.

CHAPTER ELEVEN

Can You Be Your Best in Parenthood?

A certain daughter had two parents. And the mother said, "Daughter, excuse me from the responsibility that falls to me, I must divide my time among greater matters."

Not many days later, she gathered all opportunities together and invested herself in many activities. And she became respected in community service, successful in a new career, and popular in social circles of play and pleasure.

And when she had spent herself in many splendid tasks, there arose a great famine in her soul. And she joined herself to new friends and new clubs and would fain have filled her hungry heart with pleasures and popularity, but nothing satisfied.

Then she came to herself and said, "How many of my acquaintances have the love of their daughters, while I perish, empty and unfulfilled for want of her love? I will arise and go to my daughter, and will say to her. . .'Daughter, I have sinned against heaven, against parenthood, and against you. I'm no more worthy to be called your mother. . .but let me be one of your friends.' "

So the mother arose hastily and came to her daughter, and said, "Daughter, I have sinned, I am unworthy to be called your mother. Make me one of your friends."

But the daughter said. . ."Where were you when I needed you? You have waited too long. Go back to your own fun and your oh-so-very-important jobs. I get along better without you—stranger. You are too late."

Now the father came in from his businesses at that moment, he heard the daughter's words to her mother, and in anger he said, "Daughter, we have given you everything you ever asked, all the money, gifts, liberty. . .and what more could you possibly wish for?"

And the daughter said. . ."I asked for parents. But you, my parents, were lost, and would not be found." (Paraphrase from Luke 15:11-32.)

Who is prodigal? Who is delinquent?

Yes, there have been many prodigal sons who turned their backs on father and mother *"to waste their own lives in riotous living" (Luke 15:13).*

But what of prodigal parents? Parents who waste not only their own lives, but also the lives entrusted to their responsibility—their children.

How does one become a prodigal parent?

It's simple. Just don't give yourself to your child.

Keep your schedule too full with outside-the-home activities to spend time playing, and just being with him.

Keep your mind too full with outside plans and ideas to give time listening to him.

Keep your heart too full of outside-the-home loyalties and responsibilities to have time for loving him.

Keep your relationship with him simple. Don't get too deeply involved. That takes time, energy, understanding, and insight that should be going into your business or profession. Don't try to understand him, you probably couldn't anyway. Why waste the effort? And don't get involved in discipline. Why antagonize the child? Keep on his good side. Give him everything he wants. You can always make up for anything with a few more presents.

That is a surefire formula guaranteed to produce both prodigal children and parents. . .and children's children. It's absolutely guaranteed, in God's own law—the Ten Commandments. Remember? Or haven't you read the fine print guarantee attached to the first four commandments. May I quote this one?

"For I the Lord thy God am a jealous God, visiting the iniquity of the fathers upon the children unto the third and fourth generation of them that hate me "(Exodus 20: 5).

That, tragically, is one of the laws built into our universe —and into us humans. The evil that we do, and the evil that we are comes out again and again in our children and their children in chain reaction.

The values our children learn to live by are caught, not taught. They are absorbed from the matrix of the home. Just as the mother provides the prenatal matrix for an embryo to become a living individual, so the family provides the postnatal matrix for a human to become a person.

"At birth," as American educator Horace Bushnell once put it, "the child is a candidate for personality."

Yes, and it is the home which provides the essential emotional, mental and spiritual nutriments for personality and personhood. Once they said a child's personality was formed and largely set for life by the age of three. Then they moved it back to 2, then 1, then 9 months. Now some say 8 months, others 6.

Parents are people molders. They accept responsibility for a child who in his first three years will be a sensory being, predominately emotional, learning from feeling and response. So what you are, your child is becoming. Is your life worth repeating in the lives of your children?

Or does it need new guidelines, a new pattern for parenthood before it is worthy to be a pattern to children?

Children learn to live from the way their parents live. Like parents—like children. They are twice as sensitive and almost as instant as polaroid film. When we reproduce ourselves, we really do!

Parents are patterns.

Writer John Drescher describes how...

"As our child grows, he carries in his character the subtle impressions of his home. If the atmosphere is one of love, he absorbs it. If we have time for our children, we find that our children have time for us. If we express love and devotion...we build love and devotion. If we prove by our actions that we want our children today, our children will want us tomorrow."[1]

One of the indelible memories of my childhood is of a vow I made to myself one tearstained day while sitting on my favorite branch of a weeping willow tree.

I'd just been much offended by some brash adult oversight or misunderstanding, so I promised myself...

"When I get big, when I grow up, I'm gonna remember just how a child feels about this. I won't forget."

Now I'm an adult—I hope—and a parent—I know. And I still agree with that six-year-old decision. Only, for the life of me, I can't recall what it was I vowed to remember.

One thing does recur to me from childhood. The great importance of adults seeing things through children's eyes, the crucial significance of understanding what each child feels, needs and wants.

What do your children really think, feel and want? I'm not suggesting that we research it, then legislate it for all parents. We're past the point—I hope—of believing that we will ruin our offspring unless we allow them the privilege of tyranny from toddlerhood to teenage.

But realistically, our children's deeper wants and needs, if we listen for them, may have a bit more wisdom than we're willing to credit them. (They may be almost as bright as the grandparents say!)

Dr. R. F. Hertz, a British author and psychologist, recently completed a research project to discover what children really feel and want.

He interviewed 100,000 children, ages eight to fourteen, from twenty-four countries, out of varied social classes to discover a listing of ten rules for the behavior of parents.

Care to risk hearing them?

1. Do not quarrel in front of your children.
2. Treat all your children with equal affection.
3. Never lie to a child.
4. There must be mutual tolerance between parents.
5. There should be comradeship between parents and children.
6. Treat your children's friends as welcome visitors in the home.
7. Always answer children's questions.
8. Don't blame or punish your child in front of the neighbor's kids.
9. Concentrate on your child's good points, and don't over-emphasize his failings.
10. Be constant in your affection and your moods. [2]

If that's what 100,000 ten-year-old wish from their parents, then the next generation can't be all bad! In fact, seeing our own parenthood through those children's eyes is not a bad idea for us all! It could start us being genuine persons again to each other as husbands and wives; and it might startle us into recognizing our children as true persons, as the people, the actual individuals that they are!

And we might begin communicating the real values that we say we want to get through to them, the value of life, of love and of faith.

Love your children with care. They become what you are. One day we all awake to discover that our children reveal what we have unconsciously been thinking and doing all the while. We parents are patterns.

Mothers are models.

"No one is born a woman," as Simone de Beauvior says in *The Second Sex,* "one is merely born a female, she becomes a woman."[3] That is, she becomes a woman according to the models and meanings provided by home and culture. A girl, and to a large degree, a boy, models his or her identity after the mother and the mother's ideal image or value system.

The mother is the first model for any child. Or should be. By the age of three, the die is cast. The old saw "Give me a child until he's seven, and I'll mold him for life" was a gross overestimation. Most psychologists now insist that the mother has indelibly stamped his personality by the time he learns to talk.

Mothers are models. They mold for life.

Mother, you hold a life in your hands. A life you are either forming or deforming. Children are persons. They are people, too. They are of equal worth, of equal value with you. Of infinite importance.

Speaking to a college conference on "Parents and Children," author and columnist Sydney J. Harris suggested ten new commandments for parents.

1. Thou shalt honor no other gods but God, steadfastly refusing to make thy child a minor deity in thy household.

2. Thou shalt make no promises that are broken, whether these be promises of pleasure or punishment.

3. Thou shalt teach thy child by example, and not by precept, for a parent. . .must expect his conduct to be followed and his counsel ignored.

4. Thou shalt worship on the Sabbath communally with thy family, and not seek solitary pleasures when thou shouldest most be together.

5. Thou shalt not instill fears into thy child, but rather. . . love; for he who commits no wrongs because of fear is merely weak, whereas he who pursueth righteousness in love is truly strong.

6. Thou shalt help thy child accept the variety of mankind with joy and wonder in God's creative originality, and not breed in him that terrible false pride of superiority which stunts and twists the personality of man.

7. Thou shalt not be too much parent; allow thy child to make his own mistakes, and protect him not from the painful consequences of his errors.

8. Thou shalt not expect nor demand love from thy child but thou shalt win his respect as a person by justice, humor and understanding.

9. Thou shalt not force thy child to develop in thine own image, but assist him in becoming the best kind of person his own nature requires.

10. Thou shalt look daily into thine own heart and examine thy motives; for when thy motives are impure, love curdles into possessiveness, and thy child is no longer a creature of God but an instrument of man's misguided passion. [4]

Ten good rules, ten very good rules for parents who choose to reproduce more than the image and likeness of themselves—warts and all. Those are rules for parents who want to see their children grow up into a greater image, like the image of God in Jesus Christ.

Jesus Christ always had time for children. He valued them as highly as all other individuals He met. To His disciples who tried to shoo away the children who gathered, Christ said:

"You must let little children come to me, and you must never stop them. The kingdom of Heaven belongs to little children like these" (Matt. 19:14, Phillips)!

Christ saw the immeasurable impact adult influences have on children—for good or evil. He once said:

"If anyone leads astray one of these little children who believe in me he would be better off thrown into the depths of the sea with a mill-stone hung round his neck" (Matt. 18:6, Phillips)!

That's a rather strong way of making a point, but the values it teaches are forever valid.

A child is not a toy to be trifled with or a pet to be played with; he is a person to be respected, loved, taught, disciplined and built into a man. A whole man.

Parents are patterns, and mothers are models.

Fathers fulfill character.

The Bible describes it perfectly...

You will remember how. . .a father deals with each one of his own children personally, stimulating faith and courage and giving instruction. The only object. . .to help them live lives worthy of the God who has called us to share the splendor of His own kingdom (I Thessalonians 2:11, 12, paraphrase from Phillips).

> *Fathers, don't over-correct your children or make it difficult for them to obey the commandment.* [*Honour thy father and thy mother*] *Bring them up with Christian teaching in Christian discipline (Eph. 6:2b, 4, Phillips).*

Of all directives on being responsible parents, the best are found in the ten original commandments in the Bible. True, they cover the problems of man in general and speak to every area of life, and all at the same time.

But when applied to parents—they take on the fresh significance of a timeless rule found eternally true to life. May we examine the Ten Commandments (Ex. 20:1-20) as they apply to parents and parenthood.

The first: *"You shall have no other gods before me."* You shall let God be God in your home. Let Christ be the Christ. Let Him be first!

Second: *"You shall not make yourself a graven image."* You shall not let things, money, status, success, work or pleasure take first place in your life and crowd out your first loyalty to God and family.

Third: *"You shall not take the name of the Lord your God in vain."* You shall keep all pledges punctually, never violating your vows, never perjuring your promises. Be true to your word, be true to God, true to your family.

Fourth: "Remember the Sabbath day to keep it holy." Remember to keep a day of worship, a day of relaxation together, a day for mutual sharing together as true persons.

Fifth: *"Honor your father and your mother."* Honor your children with respect under God. Nuture, encourage and guide them by life and by word.

Sixth: *"You shall not kill."* You shall respect life, by teaching wholesome self-control, responsible respect for others, and reverence for all.

Seventh: *"You shall not commit adultry."* You shall not be unfaithful to your wife, to your life together, to your commitment to be a father.

Eighth: *"You shall not steal."* You shall not steal from your family the time, the attention, the love and the loyalty which is rightly theirs.

Ninth: *"You shall not bear false witness."* You shall speak the truth in every conversation, act the truth in every circumstance, be the truth in every relationship.

Tenth: *"You shall not covet."* You shall live with acceptance, with contentment, with appreciation for what you possess. You shall ignore the Joneses, reject their phony competition and live a genuine life of purpose and meaning.

Yes, old, old commandments, but who can improve on them? They are as modern as the problems of tomorrow. And as appropriate to your family as the solutions you are finding today.

If we keep them, we will become all we can be; the wholesome, truly human people God designed us to be. Men and women alive to Jesus Christ.

Speaking of Christ, remember how He summarized the Ten Commandments?

" *'Thou shalt love the Lord thy God with all thy heart,*

and with all thy soul and with all thy mind.' This is the first and great commandment. And there is a second like it: 'Thou shalt love thy neighbor as thyself'" (Matt. 22:37-39, Phillips).

"Love the Lord God with all that you are."

"Love your family as yourself."

A certain son. . .a certain daughter had two parents. And both of them said, "Children, excuse us from the responsibility that has fallen to us. . ."

And so begins the story—the tragic story—of thousands and thousands of prodigal parents. Reproducing themselves in prodigal children.

Could it be you?

Or are you giving yourself to love and listen?

Are you giving your time to understand, encourage, direct and discipline? Are you giving your life as an example of clean, wholesome character, a pattern for mature, satisfying, believable Christian living? Are you giving your faith—a credible, consistent faith for them to love and follow?

That—and only that—is parenthood.

The cost is great—the rewards even greater.

In contrast, it costs little to be a prodigal parent—until later. . .but oh the price that is paid in the end.

Which are you? Parent? Or prodigal?

CHAPTER TWELVE

Can You Be Your Best in Love?

To be all you can be—love. On that point the whole world comes to one of its desperately few points of agreement.

But try to define it, and disagreements break out all over. Who knows what "love" is?

"I have not used the word love in the last three years," a young minister told me recently. "It's too dangerous," he explained. "No one knows what it means! I only refer to concern, respect and affectionate appreciation."

Shall we silence the word "love"? It used to be said that a Scott or his wife would never tell the other of love until one of them was dying—to save the best till last.

Like the rugged old New England Yankee, sitting before the hearth with his wife of fifty years. Years of inarticulate but loyal love. Watching the firelight dance across her craggy features, he is at last overcome by emotion and ventures a word. "Marthee," he says, "sometimes I like ye so much I can hardly keep from tellin' ye!"

How much better that is than the love of a man who told

his bride, "I paid you my supreme compliment by marrying you, I can't top that, don't expect another. I told you I love you. If I ever change my mind, I'll let you know."

Such claims to love might as well be silent. Who could believe them anyway? Who could know what they truly mean?

But then, who knows what anyone means with an expresstion of love until you've seen how it acts, heard what it says, examined what it does?

The word has come to be used for such a strange admixture of meanings and emotions, a hopeless intermingling of loves—lyrical and cheap, sacred and sensual, foolish and sublime.

In his book, *Tomorrow and Tomorrow and Tomorrow,* Aldous Huxley began writing an epitaph for "love", but it came out a bit surprisingly.

Of all the worn, smudged, dog's-eared words in our vocabulary, "love" is surely the grubbiest, smelliest, grimiest. Bawled from a million pulpits, lasciviously crooned through hundreds of millions of loud-speakers, it has become an outrage to good taste and decent feeling, an obscenity which one hesitates to pronounce. And yet it has to be pronounced, for after all, love is the last word. [1]

Never was love more indispensable, more necessary to the sanity of humanity than now. When the chips are down, we all fall back to that simple affirmation, "What the world needs now is love."

As did former Harvard professor Pitirim Sorokin who gave testimony to his discoveries gleaned from spending four years on death row in a Siberian death camp, expecting each footfall of a guard outside to be the signal of his execution. He wrote in his book, *The Ways and Power of Love:*

Whatever may happen in the future I know that I have learned three things which will remain forever convictions of my heart as well as my mind. Life, even the hardest life, is the most beautiful, wonderful, miraculous treasure in the world. . .fulfillment of duty is another marvelous thing making life happy. This is my second conviction. My third is that cruelty, hatred, violence and injustice never can and never will be able to create. . .The only way. . .is the royal road of all-giving creative love, not only preached, but consistently practiced. [2]

That is what we desperately need. A love that captivates a man's heart as well as his mind. A love that moves from principle to practice.

If we say, "I agree with something in principle," we are confessing inadvertantly that we will never fulfill it in practice. We can agree with love as a wonderful solution to frictions and frustrations and yet never make a move toward experiencing it.

It is not a head knowledge of the theories of love that we need, but a heart-discovery of love that captivates us.

Vance Havner, the great Southern minister, once told of a stodgy old bachelor professor who spent thirty years researching and writing a book on love. He defined romantic love, for example, as: "A heterogeneous conglomeration of absurdity calculated to embezzle the amity of the individual, to be intoxicated and intimidate by an irresistible power." When he took the book to a typist, for the first time the old boy fell helplessly in love. And best of all, he discovered more of love in thirty minutes of experience than he had uncovered in thirty years of research!

It is the living, breathing experience of love for others that must be discovered, not some flawless theory of affections and adorations.

To become all you can be, you must break down your resistances to giving love to others, break out from the isolation of living only for yourself, and break through the barriers that keep you from giving yourself to others in loving acceptance. And that—let's face it—lies at the end of a long maturing process of growing in living-by-love.

We are born with a love vacuum, a capacity to absorb love, that is all out of proportion to our size. A child needs massive quantities of pure love applied all over him if he is to grow up a loving person.

And growth comes slowly as we ascend the ladder of love.

Rung one: I love myself for my own sake.
              (That's infancy and the drive to survive.)

Rung two: I love others for my own sake.
              (That's love of mother for milk's sake.)

Rung three: I love others for their sake.
              (That's the discovery that others are persons too, and we love them for what they are.)

Rung four: I love God for my sake, and I love God for His own sake. (But always for my sake too. We can never say we love God for His sake alone. That is to say we don't need Him, and we are always dependent in ways beyond our knowing.)

Rung five: I love my neighbor for God's sake, for my neighbor's and for my sake. (All these are interlocking and indivisible. Because God loves both me and my neighbor, I can love God and my neighbor as myself.)

Rung six: I love myself for God's sake, my neighbor's sake, and for my sake. (Again these cannot be divided. Now I can love myself but not for my own sake alone.)

Perfect maturity of love—to love God, neighbor and self in perfect balance—is exactly what Jesus demanded of us in His Sermon on the Mount. He used love for the enemy as His starting point, and the perfectly unlimited, unconditional love of God as the ending goal. Listen to His words:

"But I say to all of you who will listen to me: love your enemies, do good to those who hate you, bless those who curse you, and pray for those who treat you badly.

"As for the man who hits you on one cheek, offer him

the other one as well! And if a man is taking away your coat, do not stop him from taking your shirt as well. Give to everyone who asks you, and when a man has taken what belongs to you, don't demand it back.

"Treat men exactly as you would like them to treat you. If you love only those who love you, what credit is that to you? Even sinners love those who love them! And if you do good only to those who do good to you, what credit is that to you? Even sinners to that. And if you lend only to those from whom you hope to get your money back, what credit is that to you? Even sinners lend to sinners and expect to get their money back. No, you are to love your enemies and do good and lend without hope of return. Your reward will be wonderful and you will be sons of the most high. For he is kind to the ungrateful and the wicked!

"You must be merciful, as your Father in Heaven is merciful." (Luke 6:27-36, Phillips).

How—yes—how can we move toward maturity in love?

How can we be our best in love-as-a-way-of-life?

By doing our best in love. Love is something you do. And as you do, love becomes something that you are.

Love is first an act of the will.

Christian love is the decision of your will to act in a concerned, responsible way toward another whether you like him or not. Love is not an emotion that just comes naturally, it's an action that comes from an inner decision to follow Jesus Christ's way of helpful, self-forgetful, purposeful compassion.

It begins in the will. When I will to do Christ's will. When it is demonstrated in action, then it begins to penetrate and slowly effect a change in your feelings toward others. Yes, you will discover what it is to like the unlikable, to love the unlovely, the unloving, yes even the unlovable.

That is why Christ unhesitatingly commanded that we love. It is His new commandment. You cannot command the heart to love, but the will. The will is open to command and obedient to the authorities it recognizes as sovereign.

If you cannot find within yourself the strength to make this willing surrender of the will, you may pray, "Lord, make me willing to be willing. Bend my will until I can decide decisively, until I am willing to take Your way in life."

What difference will this make in your strength to love? I can promise nothing. But I can affirm the difference it has made in my life and the lives of many people I know and have known. Once the decision is made in the muscular stronghold of the soul, the will, I discovered that it is possible to act in a loving way toward people I had considered impossible before.

Then came the real breakthrough. A new capacity to not only act loving, but also to feel loving toward others. It was as if the strength-to-love that Jesus promised had been released through me. It was as if Jesus Christ had entered my life to be His loving self within.

That's exactly what it is. The presence of Jesus in us that makes love for unlovable people a genuine possiblity.

His Spirit—the Holy Spirit—comes into our lives with a gift of love.

His power—the power of Heaven—is available according to our need.

He is His loving self within us, and with His presence with and within us, love for others becomes possible.

The secret? Such love is dependent on the nature of the lover, not on the nature of the one loved. Such love is an attitude or action which seeks the good of the one loved rather than the good of one's own self.

How can you be and become your best in living by love?

Begin in the will. Believing that you are the object of God's love, share it. By a deliberate decision of the will.

Determine—I will act in a loving way to anyone in any situation at any cost.

Then be dependent. On Him. On His love in you. Let

Him release it in constantly growing measures.
Be all you can be — in love.

CHAPTER THIRTEEN

Can You Be Your Best in Human Relations?

"Never throw a man away," the old gentleman said, summing up his philosophy of life, "Never throw a man away, put him on the shelf. You can use him later on when you need him."

Well, that's one way of handling people!

Not long ago, a businessman said to me. . ."I make all the friends I can, everywhere I can. You never know when you'll need them or what you'll need them for. But sooner or later anyone comes in handy."

People do come in handy. When you need them. When you can use them. So you want them to always be there. Handle with care!

Or weren't people made—and meant—to be used? I mean, what are people for?

All right, let's level on it. We all use people. We use them for our own ends, use them for our own personal advantage, so what? What about this business of people-using?

How skilled we are at playing games with people as pawns.

There are social games—pit people against people or pile people on top of people so you can climb up-up-and-over. There are economic games—use people as poker chips in the gamble for success. There are personal games—use people as props, lean on them as emotional crutches. Not to mention the ways people can be used physically, sexually, mentally, religiously.

"How many good uses there are for people!" Or so we say. And what pleasure we find in our plotting and counter-plotting with people of all sorts.

But wait, I don't like being used. Neither do you. In fact, is there anything we hate much more? When I discover I'm being manipulated for someone else's advantage, when I sense that I'm being used to build another's ego, to bolster another's pride, to advance another's personal power or prestige, I don't like it. Do you?

In fact, I don't like people-users at all, and (when I catch myself at it) myself included.

People are people. Not pawns, playthings, or poker chips.

People are people. They are not usable. Collectable. Tradeable. Discardable. Forgettable.

People are perishable. People are priceless. People are irreplaceable. People are to be respected responsibly.

God made things to be used, and people to be loved. To reverse that, to love things and use people, is one of the old-est, one of the lowest, one of the most base sins known.

We were placed *in* this world to live *with* our neighbor. That's the hard part. *With* the neighbor. We'd rather be over, above, or ahead of him. Anything but live *with* him.

Check off the sins we enjoy:

Envy—jelously—is the attempt to put ourselves *in place of* our neighbor.

Pride—superiority—is the struggle to place ourselves *above* our neighbor.

Anger—hatred—is the decision to pit ourselves *against* our neighbor.

Neglect—indifference—is the intent to enjoy ourselves *without* our neighbor.

Dishonesty—deceit—is the tactic to enrich ourselves *at the expense of* our neighbor.

Betrayal—subterfuge—is the scheme to advance ourselves *behind the back of* our neighbor.

Lust—adultery—is the shortcut to intimacy for ourselves *in spite of* the other.

Yes, anything rather than live *with*—truly with— our neighbor. So we use and abuse him.[1]

People-using is the very devil of evils! And what clever camouflages it sports. Let's slip aside a few of its many masks and examine its true features. Look closely. The face you see may be your own.

The fine art of people-using often begins in such general ways. When we want to climb past—or over—others, we may use whole groups of people. We conform to the group we want to join, and then scapegoat those we've left behind who make us feel guilty. (Have you ever sided with the majority when you really believed like the minority?) Or we cultivate friendships with those who may be advantageous to us and then shun those who have nothing to offer us. (Have you ever snubbed or belittled those beneath you, or those you are indebted to just to win the approval of those attractive to you?)

But more often we use people one by one. How do we go about that?

There are the obvious ways a person may use another sexually—to gratify his own needs. (Such sexual use of others may happen most often in the mind. But that's using, too. The only difference is degree.)

Or you can use another physically, by driving them to work mercilessly when it is more to your advantage than theirs. (Such slave driving seldom benefits the slave, so guess who profits?)

Or you can use another's ability. By borrowing their ideas

and passing them off as your own—(stealing it's called). By muscling in on the opportunities and privileges which their work has earned—(thievery it's called). By exploiting another's talent to advance your own little causes.

Or there are the subtle ways we don't usually care to mention.

What is gossip but a means of pulling down those above or near you in a vain attempt to rise above them.

What is prejudice but a futile try at proving your own superiority by maligning other races or creeds.

What is cliquishness but an attempt at using the unity of a few friendships to crowd out the competition of others.

What is criticism but a technique for chiseling down those you cannot reach any other way.

And what is malice but frustrated anger because you cannot use others or are being used by someone else.

And what is flattery but the art of lathering people for more painless shaving—so you can trim them for what you want—acceptance, reassurance or their admiration.

Let's take a closer look at some of these.

Like envy, for a first example.

What an unrewarding way of using people.

Any long second thoughts will reveal how sterile, how fruitless jealousy is.

Every other temptation offers a certain measure of satisfaction in its early stages, a certain flush of enjoyment, at least for the moment. But not jealousy. Jealousy is absolutely without gratification in every stage of its slow, cancerous development.

There is no gratification in the secret satisfaction you feel at another's misfortune; nor in the exquisite delight at a competitor's downfall; nor in the exhilaration of recognizing an obvious or not-so-obvious fault in another; nor in the fulfillment of chipping away at another's reputation; nor in the pleasurable sensation of reading the name of that person you envy in the bankrupt scandal sheet, or better yet, in the obituaries.

Bittersweet rewards, at best. Bitter even as you experience them. The reason is obvious. Envy is pain. It's a slow burning in the soul that sears a man with inferior fears at the start, then fires his desires for damaging the other, flames into hostility and blind anger that resists all quenching. It hurts like poison all the way.

Yes, like poison, the poisons of malice at another's success, resentment at his good fortune, anger at his advancement.

Solomon, the ancient Jewish philosopher king, once wrote, "A tranquil heart is the life of the flesh; but jealousy is the rottenness of the bones" (Prov. 14:30 A.S.V.)

And an envious spirit serves a second helping of bitters. The envious man unconsciously recognizes the superiority of the other and this inflames his passions even more.

Could this be why jealousy is the sin we never confess, the fault we refuse to face? We own up to pride, lust, anger, or most other emotions but jealousy? Never!

Oh we may say in a complimentary way, "How wonderful, I envy you," but of course, we don't.

When we feel real live envy, we don't talk of it. Usually we lapse into silence, eyes glinting green, the claws of our discontent covered with the smooth fur of friendliness and the soft purr of false kindness.

To own up to jealousy is to admit defeat, inferiority and helpless inadequacy; it's a rare and unusual person who will admit—even to himself—the superiority of a competitor. And that is where jealousy hits us hardest. In competition. Jealousy is the competitive sin.

It's the competition of people climbing over people and personality trampling under personality.

Jealousy is the fruit of the one totally competitive root. Pride. The second common motivation for using people.

"Pride is essentially competitive—is competitive by its very nature—while the other vices are competitive only, so to speak, by accident," writes C.S. Lewis in his book, *Mere*

Christianity. He explains: "Pride gets no pleasure out of having something, only out of having more of it than the next man. We say that people are proud of being rich, or clever, or good looking, but they are not. They are proud of being richer, or cleverer, or better looking than others."[2]

When pride is frustrated, or defeated in competition, jealousy is born. And we dream of ways to rise above that successful competitor. Then malice shows its face.

So Cain plots to murder Abel, so King Saul eyes David whose success is a threat to his throne, and so men plotted to execute Jesus the Christ. Or didn't you recall that the motive for Christ's execution was jealousy? Pilate the judge recognized it as such. The record reads, "For [Pilate] knew very well that the Jewish leaders had arrested Jesus out of envy because of His popularity with the people" (Matt. 27: 18, *Living Gospels*).

However—whenever—wherever—or whyever it is done, using people is abusing people.

There are no justifications for it. People are persons to be respected. Responsibly.

Listen to this style of life. It's completely other!

Don't be selfish; don't live to make a good impression on others. Be humble, thinking of others as better than yourself. Don't just think about your own affairs, but be interested in others too and in what they are doing (Phil. 2:3, 4, Living Letters).

Love is very patient and kind, never jealous or envious, never boastful nor proud, never haughty nor selfish nor rude. Love does not demand its own way. It is not irritable or touchy. It does not hold grudges and will hardly even notice when others do it wrong. It is never glad about injustice, but rejoices whenever truth wins out. If you love someone you will be loyal to him no matter what the cost. You will always believe in him, always expect the best of him, and always stand your ground in defending him (I Cor. 13:4-7).

Little children, let us stop just saying we love people; let us really love them, and show it by our actions. If anyone says, "I love God," but keeps on hating his brother, he is a liar; for if he doesn't love his brother who is right there in front of him how can he love God Whom he has never seen? And God Himself has said that one must not only love God, but his brother too (I John 3:18; 4:20, 21, Living Letters).

That's a different kind of life—a totally different sort of living. It's a giving kind of life that lives for others, instead of assuming all others live for you and your sake.

It's the kind of life that begins when a man pledges himself to love God—heart—soul—strength—mind, and to love his neighbor as himself.

When a man cares about people—that way—then things change! Then he has no use for people. Then he begins accepting people as people. Respecting people as persons. All people. All persons.

Then as he discovers the wisdom which comes from Jesus Christ, His gift of insight into life and understanding takes away a man's reasons for envy.

Here are the facts. Before God, we are equally poor, so there's nothing to be jealous about.

Before God we are equally rich, so we've nothing to fight over.

Before God, none of us achieve acceptance by our own brilliance, skill, personalities or good fortune. We are all equally in need of His goodness of heart which we call "grace." We are all utterly dependent on His free acceptance if we shall enter life eternal. We are equally in need of Christ, equally poor and poverty stricken in spirit.

But what is more, we are equally rich in Jesus Christ when our lives have been gifted with His new life. Can't you see what a transformation of outlook this brings to the man who comes to know and follow Christ?

He can't accept proud, envious or malicious feelings. He discounts them as pure selfishness. He discards them as unworthy of any person who is poor before His Lord and thus rich in Christ through God's generosity.

That's the change of understanding that releases us from people-using.

Then a man can begin sharing the impartial, conditional kind of love God showed when He gave Himself, in Jesus, for all men—with no exceptions. Then a man can begin sharing that kind of love—God's kind of love—with all men around him.

Only genuine love can erase rivalry, discard selfish competition, vain ambition and all the other side effects of jealousy.

The only remedy for feelings of superiority over another or disregard for the welfare of another is love. The Bible describes Christ's gift of love in these words:

Love is long-suffering, and kind; love is never envious, never boastful, never conceited, never behaves unbecomingly; Love is never self-seeking, never provoked, never reckons up her wrongs; Love never rejoices at evil, but rejoices in the triumph of Truth; Love bears with all things, ever trustful, ever hopeful, ever patient. Love never fails (I Cor. 13:4-8, 20th Century).

That is the answer to people usage in human relationships. The gift of Christ's love that comes when you pledge to love Him with all your heart, and follow Him in all of your life.

No use for people! That's the beginning point. Only love —concern—respect for every man. Every man for whom Christ died. And that's Every Man.

Say, isn't it time you called your techniques of using people by their proper names? And isn't it past time that you pledge to reject any and all people-using schemes or strategies? Isn't it the right time for you to pledge to live — and love — The Jesus Way? His is the way to not use people!

CHAPTER FOURTEEN

Can You Be Your Best When Mistreated?

Can you be your best when facing an angry man?

Hostility can be a frightening thing when you see it in another man's eye. When he's giving you the eye.

How do you react? Or do you respond?

Facing hostility can bring out a man's worst in a moment's tension or a hostile situation can bring out a man's best. The crucial question is—can he face another's anger without becoming infected himself? And that calls for both self-understanding and the ability to be understanding with others.

Understanding one's own hostilities begins with the recognition that hostility is a part of our human makeup.

Dr. Leon Saul, psychiatrist and author, writes,

I believe man's hostility to man is the central problem in human affairs. . .that it is a disease to be cured and prevented like cancer, TB, or smallpox, and that its cure will result in healthier, better living—not only for society in general but for each individual in particular.[1]

Hostility, when it becomes chronic and frequently uncontrollable, is a disease. When it always lies just beneath the surface, constantly making a person irritable, touchy, critical, scapegoating or angry with an impotent rage that's fueled by everything and flares up over nothing, it's an illness. When anger is used to accomplish childish goals or to bulldoze through normal conflicts where cooperation, compromise and understanding should be enough to solve the problem, it is an illness.

It's an illness when it turns in on oneself in self-hatred, depression, or contemplated self-destruction.

When you spot such chronic symptoms in a friend, you know that he is a troubled person. That's why he is habitually making trouble for others. And this should call forth a double measure of understanding, acceptance and forgiveness from you.

If you sense such symptoms in yourself, then look for an understanding counselor. True, everyone must live with his own hostilities, but not with angry feelings such as those. You can find release, and a new life.

But, of course, owning up to your own hostilities or helping a friend face up to his is a difficult and dangerous business. All too many people totally refuse to face their inner angers. So they bottle it up and hope that it will somehow improve with age.

"Repression" it's called.

When they feel an anger-danger-signal, they smile sweetly outside and inside quickly shoo the tiger back into his cage and soothe it with a "sh. . .nice kitty. . .kitty."

But the tiger of anger won't be shushed so easily. He growls long and low in resentment, burns with bitterness.

Repressed anger hurts and keeps on hurting. If you always deal with it simply by holding it firmly in check, or sweeping it under the rug, without any form of release or healing, it can produce emotional rigidity, apathy and coldness in personality.

Even worse, hostilities pushed down into the depths of

consciousness, often ferment into depression, anxiety and eventually breakdown.

Or repressed anger comes out indirectly in critical attitudes, scapegoating, or irritableness. Often "good people" who harbor hostility will do indirectly and unconsciously what "bad people" do directly and deliberately. Unreleased, buried anger colors and contorts their motives.

Repression is an unwholesome and potentially dangerous way of dealing with anger. But if that is the only choice, it's certainly better than venting your venom on everybody else. And it's safer for both you and them.

But there is a third alternative. If expressing our anger in violent emotion is too dangerous. And repressing our anger is too disastrous. Then we must learn confessing.

Anger and hostility must be drained off in some way or another. And talking it out is one of the very few emotional safety valves we humans have.

Confessing our anger—in conversation with a counselor, or in communication with the person who is involved—can be a step toward release.

Now then, as you face a friend who is in the grip of angry emotions, how can you best be of help?

Understanding your own anger can help your control so that your own reaction does not add fuel to his fire. And self-understanding should increase your sympathy to others who still fall easy prey to their glands.

But the most significant step in maturing is moving from reacting to anger with anger to responding to hostility with heartfelt love.

When you no longer react, can you begin responding? Constructively. Creatively.

Life is an adventure through years of hostile wastelands. Not of mountains and deserts, but of craggy people and deserted lives.

Life is conflict. Conflict upon conflict. The person who is able to respond creatively discovers a whole new dimension of richness in friendships.

Conflict can be creative. It can be used creatively to make better, richer, more complete persons of both man and woman.

How we face, accept and understand conflict makes the crucial difference. Instead of such difficulty causing a breakdown of relationships, it can be the means to a breakthrough to new intimacy and understanding.

If! If we are willing to understand, to learn, to practice the art of making our conflict creative, not catastrophic. The two options — to create or to destroy — are always open before us.

Erich Fromm, the noted psychoanalyst, has written, "The man who cannot create, wants to destroy."

Few people know it, but French General Napoleon really wanted to be a writer. When his essays and stories were ridiculed by his teachers, he turned to a career of soldiery. Instead of making the world a lovelier place with words, he destroyed it with cannon and army.

As a boy, Adolph Hitler wanted to paint, but his attempts at art and beauty met only rebuke. So he turned to anger and aggression. The creative urges of beauty, love, understanding, and empathetic communication, when thwarted, turn automatically to hostility. This happens not only in major decisions of life, but again and again in the decisions of every day.

And it happens habitually in working relationships, in friendships and in marriage. When the competition of two contrasting persons and personalities produce conflicts, they tend to be disastrous. Unless, creatively, we let conflict be constructive. Where do we begin?

By realizing that maturity is not a state marked by the absence of conflict, nor is conflict any indication that maturity is absent.

By recognizing that too often the real conflicts come out indirectly over substitute issues, and eventuate in stalemate because the central differences between humans do not come into the open.

By recognizing that the real conflicts which can be used creatively and constructively are the difficulties and differences that we hide and hesitate to face, since they are threatening to our own comfort and well-being.

By seeking to understand the real issues of difference between friends or even marriage partners, and dealing honestly with them in both conversation and action.

By risking deeper conflict in opening up the actual differences, not for argument or combat, but for a venture into intimacy. (Our longing for intimacy with another can lead us to substitute a false togetherness by avoiding all threatening issues, tiptoeing around each other like ballet dancers walking on eggs.)

How do we use conflict creatively?

By facing, understanding, accepting and resolving our differences constructively.

But where do we find the strength for such a life style, for such a fundamental commitment to being creative right at the point where we naturally and inevitably tend to be destructive?

We were meant to discover lives of creative beauty, of constructive worth. We who are expressions of the Creator's creativity were created to be co-workers in His own creativity, turning the tragedies of this world into triumphs.

As the Bible describes our role in expressing God's creativity in life:

God, who is rich in mercy
Because of His great love for us,
Gave us the gift of life
Together with Christ
Thus He shows for all time
His great generosity, grace and kindness
Expressed towards us in Christ Jesus.
What we are, we owe

To the touch of His creativity
For we are His workmanship
His poems, His creative expressions
Created anew in Christ Jesus
To lives of goodness and good deeds
Which God planned before
For us to do (Author's paraphrase, Eph. 2:5, 7, 10).

Now, how does this emerge in life: In difficulty, in conflict?

It appears as an eagerness to face the hardships of life and see how they can be resolved into new meaning and strength.

Listen again to the Bible's advice:

When all kinds of trials and temptations crowd into your lives, my brothers, don't resent them as intruders, but welcome them as friends! Realise that they come to test your faith and to produce in you the quality of endurance. But let the process go on until that endurance is fully developed, and you will find you have become men of mature character with the right sort of independence. And if, in the process, any of you does not know how to meet any particular problem he has only to ask God—who gives generously to all men without making them feel foolish or guilty—and he may be quite sure that the necessary wisdom will be given him (James 1:2-5, Phillips).

But does it work in life? Does it work! Yes, yes it does.

Those who commit themselves to loving others both because of what they are, and in spite of what they aren't, discover the first step toward the spring of daily creativity— unconditional love.

And those who commit themselves to be loyal to others won't let differences create distance, they turn them into new levels of understanding.

And those who share a common loyalty—an absolute allegiance to Jesus Christ, discover not only the union of common faith, but the communion of sharing in a common strength to love, to forgive and to be forgiven. This is possible because they share common experiences of inner change and transformation through the Holy Spirit which gives an uncommon meaning in life.

All this through the creative Spirit of Christ. His Spirit, the Bible says, brought the entire creation out of a universe of chaos.

His Spirit brings a new creation into being in any man's life—when and if he responds in faith.

And His Spirit can provide the creative strength to make life's understandings and misunderstandings sparkle with constructive growth, if we follow Him in all of life.

Can your life be an expression of His creativity? Even in the face of hostility?

When you determine "yes," you will have taken a major step toward being your best.

CHAPTER FIFTEEN

Can You Be Your Best in Forgiveness?

Can you be your best in forgiving?

Major Walter Reder was an officer in the Nazi, German occupation forces controlling northern Italy during World War II. When the allies overran Italy and "liberated" it, Major Reder was captured and imprisoned.

After a quarter century behind bars, Major Reder requested a pardon so that he could return to Germany for his last years.

Italian justice officials considering his request ruled that his plea would be granted only if the survivors of the villages in which Major Reder directed the massacre of over 1,800 civilians were to vote in favor of giving their old enemy forgiveness.

The major decided to try. At the first town, Marzabotto, 288 survivors showed up at the polls. Six favored forgiveness. Two weeks later the villagers of Vinca and San Terenza Monti flooded the polls. And not one — not one — voted for forgiveness.

Would you have forgiven him? Could you have forgiven a man who had personally and coolly administrated the deaths of hundreds of your friends and neighbors? Or is that too great an evil for human forgiveness? If so, how large would your forgiveness come? For small sins only? Or medium-size iniquities?

Why ask for sizes? Because all too many of us forgive only when the injury is small enough to be forgotten, or overlooked, or simply avoided.

Consequently, we never forgive. Not really. We avoid it like the plague. No, not by outright denials. Not with a "I'll never forgive that man," but with carefully executed games. Games we play in phony forgiveness. Games that provide bargain pardons and costless forgivenesses. Shortcuts that bypass the pain of genuine forgiving.

So common are these little strategems, and so prevalent is their use that even in a public assembly of Christian people only a small percentage has any inkling of what forgiveness is all about. To be honest, forgiveness is especially rare among "good Christian people."

The late Thomas Lomax Hunter, a popular columnist in the Richmond (Virginia) *Times-Dispatch,* once wrote,

If ever I enjoy the constitutional right of trial by jury, I trust that it will not be a jury of good men. Good men, in the sense in which the word is generally understood, have so little sympathy with bad men; are so seldom kind. Being good men themselves, they think the law should make everybody else good. In a long experience as a lawyer I have always struck off good men from the jury when I had the opportunity. Good men are convictors.[1]

An exaggeration, of course (I hope), but all too often borne out in the unforgiving, unmerciful, unloving attitudes of perfect people who think all others should be made in their own image and cannot forgive them for being different.

"There are only two kinds of people in our world," suggests one observer, "the good and the bad—and the good decide which are which."

Why must so many "good" people be such judgmental, such critical, such condemning creatures?

Could it be they know little or nothing of forgiveness? Can it be that they prefer the self-protective games of false forgiving?

Why these games? Because good people claiming maturity are usually too nice, too proud, too concerned about their reputation and rapport with others to ever give a flat refusal to any request for forgiveness. So they play games. I was one of these game-loving-good-people. Perhaps you've done a bit of it too.

Game one in phony forgiveness: play-school.

"Yes, I'll forgive," its players say, "but first I'll teach him a thing or two." "Of course I'll forgive, but first he's got to know how much he's hurt me!"

The benefits of the game? It lets the player postpone forgiving. It gives him a seemingly justifiable way of getting even with the other person in a subtle, excusable way.

Some people do it in the way they accept another's apology, using the moment when the other person is vulnerable to rub a bit of salt into the bleeding sores. ("Of course I'll forgive you even though you'll never know how much it's hurt me. . .", etc.)

Others do it by continuing to drop little reminders of how badly they've been treated, how deeply they've been cut. It allows them to collect a pint or two of sweet sympathy even while they slice the victim to ribbons.

"Teaching a thing or two first" is not forgiveness. It's either a demand for justice—if you've anything coming, or worse, it's a groping for revenge. Like the dentist who turned from the phone in great enjoyment. "What's that all about?" his secretary asked. "Remember the plumber we called when our heat was off last winter—the guy who made us wait and freeze for two days? Well he just called for help on a broken tooth. I'm letting him wait three!"

Forgiveness is no game of play-school. It is not a form of "teaching another," it is a way of "accepting the other." Once we begin using it as school, it soon degenerates to a "take that. . .and that. . .and that" game of checkers or chess where you outmaneuver the other to show him what's what.

But forgiveness is a gift. A free gift of love. And a gift does not depend on the nature of the receiver but on the giver. A gift is not given to one who has earned it — then it becomes a payment. A gift is given to the undeserving. Because of the giver's love.

Jesus did not play-school-with-forgiveness. At the place of a skull, as He was being brutally handled, thrown to the cross beam, nailed wrist to wood, and then jerked roughly into the excruciating hanging torture of crucifixion, He prayed again. . .and again, "Father, forgive. Father, forgive them. Father, forgive them for their ignorant, blind brutality. Father, forgive!" (See Luke 23:32-34.)

Game two in false forgiveness: monopoly

"I'll forgive," the players say, "but when he's made it right." "Yes, I'll forgive, but when He's proven himself to me, when it's clear that he's truly sorry, when it's obvious that he's repented."

The benefits of the game? You can justify all sorts of unforgiving attitudes by saying, "Until he's made a good apology, I don't need to be loving and accepting." You can feel superior and patronizing in criticizing and correcting the other in an attempt to convert him. And best of all benefits you can quote Jesus to justify yourself.

"Didn't Jesus say, 'If your brother offends you, take him to task about it, and if he is sorry, forgive him' [Luke 17:3, Phillips]?" a man once asked me, justifying his unforgiving game. Yes, I replied, but check the verses both before and after. "Don't allow yourself to cause anyone to stumble and fall in any way," Jesus said in preface to that instruction and then in following He added:

Yes, if [your brother] wrongs you seven times in one

day and turns to you and says, 'I am sorry' seven times,
you must forgive him" (Luke 17:4, Phillips).

"Seven times in one day!" That's ample evidence that the man is not truly repentant. And then he has the brass to come back asking for your forgiveness every hour on the hour. Yet you forgive him, said Jesus. No game playing there.

Another time when the same question arose, Jesus took the matter even further. Then Peter approached Him with the question,

"Master, how many times can my brother wrong me and I must forgive him? Would seven times be enough?"
"No," replied Jesus, "not seven times, but seventy times seven" (Matt. 18:21-11, Phillips)!

The real problem with playing monopoly in forgiveness is that it's another bold demand for repayment. We pull for the other to repent not for his sake, but so we can get some satisfaction from his discomfort to solve our own hurt feelings.

But even though we may have a monopoly on forgiveness, even though all the cards may be in our hand, we can never get any repayment that satisfies our need for justice (except when stolen things are repaid) or that satisfies our need for revenge.

The man who demands justice or revenge is unforgiving in heart, and the Great Forgiver will not be able to forgive him. Or so Jesus said. (See Matt. 18:2)

Game three in fraudulent forgiveness: charades, let's pretend.

"Yes, I'll forgive," its players say, "we'll just act like it never happened. I'll just pretend that we're turning the clock back to the time before it all happened. I'll just forget it and erase it all from my mind."

The benefits of the game? It lets you avoid facing the real hurt between you and the other person. It lets you deny all your anger without going through the painful process of working it out in honesty.

Disadvantages? The real problem of injury between you and your offender is still there. It is only repressed into some dark closet of your memory. The anger still festers away in your inner system. The barrier of grudge, resentment or bitterness still stands.

Anger can't be simply avoided. It must be faced, confessed and expressed, and that is no game of pretense.

And the final difficulty. It's impossible. In spite of your skill at acting otherwise, we can't pretend our troubles away. They can't be forgotten at will. They have a way of walking through our memory by night. And by day.

In any injury, there is anger on two sides. For the offender, there is the anger that may have caused the original hurt and now the anger at being caught in a situation where he is at another's mercy. For the injured party, there is the justifiable anger at what has been done to him. To pretend that these emotions never existed is to deny reality. They must be dealt with.

If the injured party intends to demand justice, he releases his anger on the person who injured him and obtains satisfaction. (Legally, there is never any true satisfaction in justice because we ourselves are never truly just, innocent and free from the constant need for the mercy and forgiveness of others. So even while we're extracting justice from another, we are well aware of our own hidden needs for the mercy and love of both God and man.)

If the injured party forgives, he consciously bears his own anger, and decisively sets the offender free. In so doing he pays the cost of forgiving. All forgiveness is costly. Forgiving us cost God—Calvary!

In every act of evil and injury, someone must pay. No debt is ever canceled without someone bearing the loss. No gift is ever made without someone bearing the cost. So it is in forgiveness. Someone always pays. Either the offender pays—that's justice. Or the offended substitutes himself in payment—that's forgiveness. Or one or both play games and both pay unconsciously through hidden means with fantastic interest rates of bitterness, resentment and personality decay. And finally they cut themselves off from the forgiveness of God.

"Forgive us what we owe to you, as we have also forgiven those who owe anything to us," said Jesus in the prayer He taught us to pray.

Afterward Christ added:

*"For if you forgive other people **their** failures, your Heavenly Father will also forgive you. But if you will not forgive other people, neither will your Heavenly Father forgive you your failures" (Matt. 6:12, 14, 15, Phillips).*

Game four in false forgiveness: king of the mountain.

"Of course, I'll forgive," the player says. "Why he couldn't have hurt me. It was nothing at all. And who does he think he is to come apologizing to me? His acts mean nothing at all. Not to me!"

Benefits? It provides a man the perfect safety of withdrawal from a painful situation. It offers him the superior feelings of pride. It lets him put the other person down under the guise of generosity.

But is that truly the case? Yes, there may be situations in which a hypersensitive person comes with apology in hand and you honestly can't recall the offense he is referring to. But then you have no defenses. And you tend to accept his words at their face value.

But when we play king-of-the-mountain by mouthing any of the you-couldn't-have-hurt-me, we are confessing inadvertently that we have been hurt and we are indeed hurting yet. But rather than admit it and deal with our anger and injury we retreat into unapproachable goodness.

Or is it haughty superiority like the giant ox in Aesop's fable who had just received an apology from a gnat riding his horn? "I do hope I haven't burdened you with my weight," the gnat said. "I quite forgot that it may have been an inconvenience to you." "On the contrary," the ox replied, "I was quite unaware that you were there."

Forgiveness happens truly between equals. A truly forgiving person offers acceptance and love out of an awareness that he too is in constant need of the forgiveness of God.

He does not condone the evil by saying, "Oh it was nothing, nothing at all." To condone an evil is simply to ignore it, to treat it as if it were good. But forgiveness recognizes the evil as evil, accepts one's own anger at the act and its results, and sets the other free from indebtedness so that he can live again in healing and health.

For forgiveness to be complete, it must be both offered and accepted. But the forgiver has control over only one side of that. He can be a healing force, seeking to mend the breach and close the wound, but he cannot bring the other to acceptance. He can only love him toward it.

Notice how St. Paul describes what forgiving should be.

Let there be no more resentment, no more anger or temper, no more violent self-assertiveness, no more slander and no more malicious remarks. Be kind to each other, be understanding. Be as ready to forgive others as God for Christ's sake has forgiven you (Eph. 4:31-32, Phillips).

As, therefore, God's picked representatives of the new humanity, purified and beloved of God himself, be merciful in action, kindly in heart, humble in mind. Accept life, and be most patient and tolerant with one another, always ready to forgive if you have a difference with anyone. Forgive as freely as the Lord has forgiven you. And, above everything else, be truly loving, for love is the golden chain of all the virtues (Col 3:12-14, Phillips).

That is forgiveness. As Christ gives it. Costly forgiveness—it costs the forgiver exactly what the hurt is and has done. Substitutional forgiveness—it asks the forgiver to substitute himself for the offending party and bear his own anger at the evil and the evildoer. Unconditional forgiveness —that is forgiveness not on any human conditions, but only on the conditions of love shown us in Jesus and the way of Calvary. Healing forgiveness—that seeks to restore right relationships with the one who has broken the friendship.

All games aside—why not be all you can be—in forgiving.

CHAPTER SIXTEEN

Can You Be Your Best in Joy?

Can you find happiness?

Or is happiness a will-o'-the-wisp that eludes a man's grasp from cradle to coffin?

Or when a man begins that lifelong journey toward maturity, can he also be all he can be in genuine happiness?

For so many people, happiness is always just beyond their out-stretched fingertips.

"Just when we'd paid off our property and had enough saved up to enjoy ourselves," his wife told me today, "just when we were ready to be happy, then John had this stroke . . . ."

"Just when the children were married and gone, and we had met all our obligations," a man told me last week, "just when we were ready to find happiness, then came my wife's cancer."

A young man recently told me: "I'd just sweated my way through high school, (what a drag) then got me this good job, a sharp car. . .and then when I think I've got happiness on a string, I get drafted. . .and come back with no legs."

I can't forget the businessman who said: "I was just reaching security in my business; I'd been working day and night for years. Sure, my wife had to make a few sacrifices, but she'd always pushed me to succeed. Now, just when we could enjoy a little well-earned happiness, she walked out on me."

Just when we were ready to be happy. . .

Just when we had earned a little happiness. . .

Just when we were financially able to be happy. . .

Strange how tragedy intervenes, just as we're ready to let happiness begin. Or is it some other circumstance? There's always something or other.

Or even more strange, when nothing intervenes, how happiness somehow eludes our search, our drive to seize it. We pursue it, but never quite capture it. And all the time we thought it was one of our "unalienable American rights."

Ashley-Montagu, anthropologist and social critic, writes:

The pursuit of happiness in America is perhaps the most misconceived of human endeavors. Life and liberty are indeed necessities, but the pursuit of happiness is a fool's game, a will-o'-the-wisp that eludes all who believe that by making it a goal, they can, by the prescribed or some other means, achieve it. The truth is—and it is a sad truth—that happiness cannot be pursued and caught like a butterfly in a collector's net.

The truth is that it is not the purpose of a human being's life—to be happy. The moments of happiness we enjoy take us by surprise. It is not that we seize them, but that they seize us. It is the state when one is least conscious of oneself that one is likely to be one's happiest. It is not so much the pursuit of happiness, but the happiness of pursuit.[1]

Certainly there are elements of truth in all that. . .the first is. . .Happiness is essentially and inevitably a by-product, that comes invariably by indirection.

"Make it the object of your pursuit and it leads you on a wildgoose chase," said Nathaniel Hawthorne, the early American author.

The best things of life are by-products, side-effects, the fruits of other labor.

Set your heart on them, go all out for them and they elude you.

You may pursue honors, but you must earn honor!

You may pursue reputation, but you must win respect!

You may achieve affluence, but you must merit influence!

To strive for a striking personality is disastrous, artificial, self-conscious. It is not when we attempt to impress others that we impress them most. Nothing on earth makes happiness more unapproachable than trying to find it.

Happiness is the by-product of a life wholly given to the pursuit of something greater. But what is this "something greater"?

"No one is born happy," say some thinkers. "It is something that comes to you, it is brought about by inner productiveness and meaning found in a great life-task."

"The happiest person," said Timothy Dwight, onetime president of Yale University, "is the person who thinks the most interesting thoughts."

William McDougall, one of the world's most respected psychologists, expands this thought by saying: "The richer, the more highly developed, the more completely unified or integrated is the personality, the more capable it is of sustained happiness, in spite of intercurrent pains of all sorts."

One of our large daily newspapers recently offered a prize for the best answer to the question: "Who are the happiest people on earth?"

The prize-winning answers that were considered best:

—a mother bathing her baby at the end of a busy day.

—a craftsman whistling over a job well done.

—a little child building castles in the sand.

—a doctor who has just finished a difficult operation and saved a human life.

Each person was so absorbed in the meaning of the task at hand that each one forgot himself. And they were overtaken by joy.

Historian Will Durant once confessed that he had sought happiness in knowledge, and found only disillusionment. He then looked for happiness in travel and found weariness; in wealth, but found discord and worry. He looked for happiness in his writing and was only fatigued.

One day he saw a woman waiting in a tiny car with a sleeping child in her arms. A man descended from the train, gently kissed her, softly kissed the baby, so as not to awaken him, then they drove off happily together. Then it struck him. Happiness is found in life for others!

Jesus gave us a flawless portrayal of the man enroute to maturity who discovers happiness happening all along the way. It's a very penetrating portrayal—typical of Jesus—that examines attitudes, motives, and values in living. It's found in the Beatitudes that introduced His Sermon on the Mount.

Let's examine them individually for clues toward discovering happiness. (Matt. 5:3-10, Phillips).

Jesus said:

"How happy are the humble-minded, for the kingdom of Heaven is theirs!"

Happiness is—the honesty to see my own inability, and humility to seize upon His ability, for then His kingdom is mine.

I lived for ten young years, trying to prove my ability by high achievements, to demonstrate my insights by clever speech, to show my brilliance by deep doubts. Slowly I came to realize that the deepest doubts I should have were doubts about my own self-sufficiency, the sharpest insights I could have were insights into my own inadequacies, and the greatest ability needed was usability in service to God, and responsibility in obedience to Christ! Happiness is honesty —humility.

Jesus said:

"How happy are those who know what sorrow means, for they will be given courage and comfort!"

Happiness is—the sensitivity to suffer with the tragedies about me, for out of sorrow comes courage, confidence and comfort.

Happiness is sensitivity to suffering and sorrow? Yes, it's a suffering world. Go ahead, let it tear at your heart a little. Begin to feel, begin to live. Begin to ask God, "Let my heart hurt with the hurts of men. Let it bleed with the tragedies of all men. Let my heart be broken with the things that break Your heart, O God!" Happiness is sensitivity to sorrow and joy!

Jesus said:

"How happy are those [of a gentle spirit] for the whole earth will belong to them!"

Happiness is—the discipline of gentleness and generosity; for then His whole earth is my homeland, my inheritance.

Happiness is the discipline of gentleness and generosity? Yes. Only the disciplined are free—free to live as true men and women. Truly human, truly alive to others. Truly loving and loved. Truly serving and sharing. Happiness is gentle generosity.

Jesus said:

"Happy are those who are hungry and thirsty for goodness, for they will be fully satisfied!"

Happiness is—the aching dissatisfaction with less than the best, the hungry longing for only the highest; for then His goodness can bring fullest fulfillment.

Happiness is finding hunger, thirst and longing satisfied through Christ's new life.

Jesus said:

"Happy are the merciful, for they will have mercy shown to them!"

Happiness is—the sympathy to understand others, the compassion to accept others, the concern to forgive others; for the same will be received from both God and man.

Happiness is forgiveness? Yes. . .if you forgive others, you will be forgiven. If you give understanding, you will be understood. If you give acceptance, you will find acceptance. Give unto others as you would have them give unto you. This is happiness.

Jesus said:

"Happy are the utterly sincere, for they will see God!"

Happiness is—the integrity to live consistently, the simplicity to live sincerely; for the man who lives such a life will see God's hand in everything about him.

Happiness is the sincerity that sees God? The pure in heart see God about them when others are blind. The sincere in heart sense God in their lives even in the midst of pain when others are despairing. The single-hearted know the presence of God when others are lonely. The simple-hearted see God. This is happiness.

Jesus said:

"Happy are those who make peace, for they will be known as sons of God!"

Happiness is—being a peacemaker, making reconciliation between man and man and between man and God; because the man who makes peace does God's own work.

Happiness is peacemaking? Yes, no matter what the cost! No matter how high the price. Happiness is bringing peace between men even though you suffer for their mistakes, bear the blows of their anger, absorb the poison of their hostility and hatred. Happiness is making peace.

Jesus said:

"Happy are those who have suffered persecution for the cause of goodness, for the kingdom of Heaven is theirs!"

Happiness is—total commitment to truth, no matter what

the cost.

Happiness is—total loyalty to goodness, no matter what the outcome.

Happiness is living by inner purpose, not by outer pressures.

Happiness is having a sense of meaning, not a feeling of futility.

Happiness is relying on inner stability, not on outer security.

Happiness is realizing a life of useful service, not a life of selfish safety.

Happy persons seldom think of happiness. They are too busy losing their lives in the meaningful sacrifices of service. And in losing life, they find it. They are not asking, "What do I want of life?" but, "What is wanted of me?" "What is needed from me now?"

Remember Christ's words?

"The man who tries to save his life will lose it; it is the man who loses his life for my sake and the gospel's who will save it. What good can it do a man to gain the whole world at the price of his own soul? What can a man offer to buy back his soul once he has lost it?

"And what happiness will be yours when people blame you and ill-treat you and say all kinds of slanderous things against you for my sake! Be glad then, yes, be tremendously glad—for your reward in Heaven is magnificent. They persecuted the prophets before your time in exactly the same way" (Mark 8:35,36; Matt. 5:11, 12, Phillips).

But the person who sets out to be deliberately happy must necessarily play it safe. Before long he is playing it too safe. He stops short just at the crucial moment.

If you stop giving at the moment you feel it, you miss out on true generosity.

If you stop serving at the moment it pinches you, you miss out on sacrifice and its rewards.

If you quit loving at the moment it becomes difficult, you

133

never discover compassion.

If you refuse to forgive when injured, you never discover the grace of unconditional forgiveness.

If you hesitate to share yourself when it costs, you never discover intimate fellowship.

You stop short of happiness, you fall short of the goodness of life itself. That's the sin of it all. And don't we all do it?

Did you know that the Bible says:

There is no distinction to be made anywhere: everyone has sinned, everyone falls short of the beauty of God's plan (Romans 3:23, Phillips).

We stop, stall in our selfishness, stagnate in our safety. We miss out on the beauty of happiness. That's the way we are. All of us. We stop short of all God intended for us. We miss out.

"To miss the joy is to miss all," Robert Louis Stevenson once wrote.

There are moments when we feel just a thrill of the joy possible to us. Moments when the beauty of nature, the warmth of love, the tenderness of relationship, the rewards of work well done flush us with joy.

These moments of joy are given to us to reveal that this is the way we are meant to live. Alive with joy. If only!

If only we knew how. If only things wouldn't keep tripping us up, stopping us short. Stalling us at the crucial moment.

It is clear that our highest reaches toward joy come when we forget ourselves in service to others. That only those who give themselves forgetfully begin to reach it. Those who live in the way of Christ, loving, caring, giving, sharing, sacrificing, even suffering, begin to discover it.

Joy is a gift. A gift of love. It comes from relationships, not things. It doesn't come "just when you are ready to settle down, relax and be happy."

Joy breaks over us when we surrender ourselves unhesitatingly to the God-who-loves-us, Jesus Christ.

Joy washes through us when we give ourselves unreservedly in loving obedience and eager willingness to live Christ's way.

Joy surprises us when we sacrifice our own safety, security, and sure success to show Christ's love to all those about us, to share Christ's kind of life with all those we know and love.

Joy is a gift. Happiness is a happening-with-God.

Be all you can be. Be joyfully His!

NOTES

Chapter 4

[1]As quoted in *Christianity Today*, July 19, 1968, p. 5, in the article "How to Be Good—and Mad," by Norman V. Hope.

Chapter 5

[1] Roy Keim, *The Mature Person,* Mennonite Hour Home Bible Studies, Lesson Five.

Chapter 6

[1] *The Meaning of Persons,* Paul Tournier, Harper and Row, New York, 1957, p. 129.

Chapter 7

[1] *Discipline and Discovery,* Albert Edward Day, The Parthenon Press, Nashville, Tennessee, 1961, p. 20.

Chapter 8

[1]Publicity materials from Pennsylvania Life Insurance Company, Los Angeles, California.
[2] *The New Dictionary of Thoughts,* Tryon Edwards, Standard Book Co., 1965, p. 645.
[3] Quoted by Ann Landers, Publishers Newspaper Syndicate.

Chapter 10

[1] Gibson Winter, *Love and Conflict: New Patterns in Family Life* (Garden City, New York, Doubleday, 1958). p. 115.

[2] As quoted by Dwight Harvey Small, *After You've Said I Do,* Revell, 1968, p. 12.

[3] Erich Fromm, *The Art of Loving* (Harper and Row, New York, 1956), p. 103.

Chapter 11

[1] John Drescher, "Like Parents, Like Children," *Mennonite Brethren Herald,* Jan. 6, 1967, p. 4.

[2] Halford E. Luccock and Robert E. Luccock, *Pulpit Digest,* Meredith Corp., Manhasset, N.Y., August, 1966.

[3] Quote by Harvey Cox, *The Secular City,* Macmillan Co., New York, 1966, p. 195.

[4] Sydney J. Harris, Newspaper Publishers Syndicate.

Chapter 12

[1] *Tomorrow and Tomorrow and Tomorrow,* by Aldous Huxley, as cited in *A Second Readers Notebook,* Harper and Brothers, New York, p. 214.

[2] *The Ways and Power of Love,* Pitirim Sorokin, cited in *A Second Readers Notebook,* Harper and Brothers, New York, p. 216.

Chapter 13

[1] I am indebted in this section to William F. May, *A Catalogue of Sins,* Holt, Rinehart and Winston, New York, 1967, p. 21.

[2] C. S. Lewis, *Mere Christianity,* Macmillan Co., New York, 1960, p. 95.

Chapter 14

[1]Leon J. Saul, *The Hostile Mind,* Random House, New York, 1956, p. 14.

Chapter 15

[1]*The Sermon on the Mount and Its Meaning for Today,* Ernest Trice Thompson, John Knox, Richmond, 1946, p. 32.

Chapter 16

[1]*The American Way of Life,* Ashley-Montague, as quoted in *The National Observer,* March 20, 1967, p. 22.

Intriguing Accounts of Life-Changing Faith

True Stories from Creation House

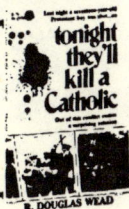